BARBARIANS *INSIDE* THE GATES

The Hoover Institution on War, Revolution and Peace, founded at Stanford University in 1919 by Herbert Hoover, who went on to become the thirty-first president of the United States, is an interdisciplinary research center for advanced study on domestic and international affairs. The views expressed in its publications are entirely those of the authors and do not necessarily reflect the views of the staff, officers, or Board of Overseers of the Hoover Institution.

www.hoover.org

Hoover Institution Press Publication No. 450

Hoover Institution at Leland Stanford Junior University,
Stanford, California 94305-6010

First printing 1999
26 25 24 23 22 21 20   15 14 13 12 11 10 9

Library of Congress Cataloging-in-Publication Data
Sowell, Thomas, 1930–
    Barbarians inside the gates—and other controversial essays / Thomas Sowell.
        p.   cm
    A collection of the author's columns from forbes magazine and from Creators Syndicate.
    Includes bibliographical references.
    ISBN 978-0-8179-9582-9 (pbk : alk. paper)
    ISBN 978-0-8179-9583-6 (epub)
    ISBN 978-0-8179-9587-4 (mobi)
    ISBN 978-0-8179-9588-1 (PDF)
    1. United States—Civilization—1970– 2. United States—Politics and government—1993– 3. United States—Social conditions—1980– 4. United States—Economic conditions—1981– I. Title.
973.92—dc21   98-33334
                               CIP

CONTENTS

Introduction   ix

PART III: **THE POLITICAL SCENE**

PART IV: **THE LEGAL SCENE**

PART V: **THE RACIAL SCENE**

PART VI: **THE EDUCATION SCENE**

PART VII: **RANDOM THOUGHTS**

INTRODUCTION

THEY SAY THAT MOST WRITERS BELIEVE that their latest book is their best, so perhaps it is inevitable that I believe this collection of my columns from *Forbes* magazine and from Creators Syndicate to be better than the three previous collections of such essays.[1] Be that as it may, what all these writings have in common is that they permit me to address a general audience without having to guard against having academics misconstrue every sentence that isn't hedged and foot-noted. In other words, common sense can be assumed when writing for the general public, though not when writing for specialists with their own hobby horses and axes to grind. If I say that the sky is blue, the average reader will understand what I mean, but clever sophisti-cates will point out that the sky is reddish at sunset, black at midnight and gray on an overcast day.

Once freed from the need to be constantly fending off the word-twisters, I find that a lot can be said in a brief essay, even on some pretty complex issues. Many laments that the public "doesn't under-stand" could more accurately be restated as "specialists have not bothered to talk in plain English." The public will not understand that two plus two equals four, if it is expressed in Chinese, but that does not mean that people are incapable of doing arithmetic.

If the title of this book suggests that I think we are facing a dire threat to the social fabric of this country, it is because I do. Some of the reasons will become apparent in the essays that follow. However, it may nevertheless be useful to make a distinction between pes-simism and despair. Those of us old enough to be privileged to have lived through the great deliverances of the twentieth century—the collapse of Jim Crow in the United States and of apartheid in South

---

[1] *Is Reality Optional?* (1993), *Compassion versus Guilt* (1987), and *Pink and Brown People* (1981)

Africa, the defeat of the Nazis on the battlefields of World War II, and the collapse of Communism in Eastern Europe—have no right to despair because our society is troubled today. Indeed, we have a duty to fight against the signs of decay and corruption around us.

Even if victory seems nowhere on the horizon, think of the all the soldiers who gave their young lives, all across this planet, during World War II, when the ultimate outcome was by no means certain and the triumph of unspeakable evil seemed very possible. Think of all those who died lonely and ugly deaths in the gulags of Siberia or in the killing fields of Kampuchea, without even a speck of dignity for themselves or a sign of hope of common decency for others in their societies.

Our task is infinitely easier than that, our dangers nothing worse than unpopularity, and our society one that has already conquered many obstacles and is capable of overcoming many more.

Finally, let me express my appreciation to Creators Syndicate, which syndicates my column to newspapers across the country, and to *Forbes* magazine, for their kind permission to reprint these columns here. A special thanks must go to Katherine Searcy of Creator's Syndicate, whose sharp editorial eye has saved me from many an embarrassing mistake. Gratitude is also owed to my research assistant, Na Liu, who has tracked down and gotten innumerable books, Census reports, scholarly articles, trade association publications, and other sources of information, and whose diligent research in libraries and on the Internet has unearthed many of the facts that I write about as if they were things I had at my fingertips all the time.

PART I
THE SOCIAL SCENE

BARBARIANS *INSIDE* THE GATES?

Is it hopeless?

That is the question that seems implicit—and often explicit—in discussions of the degeneration of American society and of Western civilization.

The signs of this degeneration are all too plain and all too widespread, from declining educational standards to high crime rates, the disintegration of families and record rates of suicide among young people. Able-bodied beggars have become a common sight in American cities from San Francisco to Washington, as well as in such foreign capitals as London and Paris.

Senator Pat Moynihan recently pointed out that handgun murders in New York City are now 30 times what they were half a century ago. Racial polarization has also become far more common on elite college campuses than it was 30 years ago, and segregated living arrangements have been created by college administrators who publicly proclaim their devotion to "diversity" almost hourly.

Perhaps worst of all, much of the degeneracy of our times is not merely tolerated but celebrated.

The ugly, ignorant and barbaric lyrics of "rap" music have been sanctified by benedictions in the columns of the *New York Times* and by Ph.D.s teaching at Ivy League universities. Multiple murderers are mourned at their executions and a child molester on the faculty of Stanford University had a medal struck in his honor after he committed suicide when confronted with his crime.

Despite a long history of struggle of blacks for better education, it has now become common in ghetto schools across the country for those black youngsters who excel academically to be denounced for

3

"acting white"—and to face social ostracism or even physical violence from their classmates.

The dangerous notion that some categories of people are guilty until proven innocent has been creeping into our legal system, along with the sophistry that double jeopardy is not double jeopardy if it is cops who were acquitted when we wanted them convicted.

The barbarians are not at the gates. They are inside the gates—and have academic tenure, judicial appointments, government grants, and control of the movies, television, and other media.

The question of the hour—and of the next century—is whether all this can be turned around.

History shows that degeneracy can be turned around because it has been done in the past. But the real question today is: Will we turn it around—or is what we are doing likely to make matters worse?

Clever sophisticates use history to show that there were alarms about crime and violence, and about the decline of the younger generation, in the past, suggesting that this shows that there is nothing to worry about. On the contrary, past lamentations were often both correct and a spur to doing something about it.

That is what turned things around.

In the early 19th century, for example, there were alarming levels of crime and degenerate behavior in American cities and in many European cities as well. What was done about it?

Massive efforts were made on many fronts to roll back the tide of barbarism. Programs to instill moral values became widespread, both in the schools and in such newly created organizations as the Young Men's Christian Association. Sunday school attendance tripled between 1821 and 1851.

The first real police forces were organized in cities across the United States and mass movements to get people to stop drinking likewise spread across the country. The per-capita consumption of alcohol, which had been going up for decades, fell by 1850 to about one-fifth of what it had been in 1829.

Not surprisingly, crime rates began to drop in the middle of the 19th century and continued to fall on into the early years of the 20th century. Studies of crime in London, Stockholm and Sydney show similar trends during the era of what the intelligentsia today refer to sneeringly as "Victorian" morality.

We have grown so used to crime, violence and other social degeneracy increasing that it may be hard to realize that improvements in all these things have occurred for long periods of time in the past.

The homicide rate in the United States declined from the time national statistics began to be collected in the early 1930s until the 1960s, when the bright ideas of the anointed began to be applied in the criminal justice system, the schools, and elsewhere in American society and in Western civilization in general.

Virtually everything that was supposed to make things better made things worse.

Worst of all, the assumptions and social dogmas of the anointed reign supreme from the schools to the colleges and in all the media. What has failed is accepted without question by so-called "thinking people" and what worked is disdained as being out of touch with the times.

No, the situation is not hopeless. But it is grim—and if nobody does anything to turn it around, it can become hopeless.

LEST WE FORGET

LIKE SO MANY PEOPLE, I regarded the Memorial Day weekend as a welcome respite from the daily grind and an opportunity for some holiday relaxation. As I was driving toward San Francisco to pursue my hobby of picture-taking, I went past a national cemetery where each grave was decorated with a small American flag, all blowing in the breeze, while larger flags flew in the background.

The peaceful beauty of the sunny scene could not hide the grim reality of endless rows of gravestones of American soldiers and sailors.

"There is the price of freedom," I thought. And I turned into the cemetery.

There were not very many people there, perhaps not nearly as many as there should have been. I had no one buried in this cemetery but I knew that I would not be alive today if it were not for those who were buried beneath the flags and the headstones.

At the first place where I stopped to take a picture, there were two gravestones near each other with the same year of birth and the same year of death—a sergeant and a lieutenant, both born in 1921 and both dead in 1944. These young lives that had been snuffed out in the carnage of war were responsible for my still being alive—and free.

Had Hitler won, I would long ago have been just a wisp of smoke coming out of a chimney in some concentration camp.

As I was trying to decide what lenses and films to use, an elderly couple—Asian, as it happened—came by with much deeper things on their minds. They were carrying flowers to one of the graves.

Here and there in the sea of gravestones, there were other people, usually in small groups, gathered around a grave of someone dear to them. One lady was sitting by herself on the grass by a grave. Another, much older, was walking toward another grave, leaning heavily on her cane.

Coming across a rise was a pretty little girl, maybe five or six years old. I wondered if anyone had told her how much she owed to these people buried here. I wondered if I would have thought about it myself if my route had not taken me past this cemetery.

In the age of "doing your own thing," many seem unwilling to acknowledge how much they owe to others, who never had a chance to do their own thing. In the sobering dignity of a military cemetery, it was hard to imagine how anyone could want to send more young people off into battle, to be cut down on the threshold of life, unless there were some very high stakes for the American people.

Those editorial-office heroes who are itching to send American troops off to the Balkans or elsewhere need to spend some time in a military cemetery, and especially to notice the terribly young ages of so many buried there. Yet some media people ask: "What is the point of being a superpower" if we are not going to take on "world responsibilities."

The point of being a superpower is so that no one will attack you and require the sacrifice of more and more young Americans like those buried in this cemetery. We were attacked at Pearl Harbor because we were sitting ducks who had allowed our military forces to dwindle away until we had a smaller army than Portugal's—and not enough equipment even for this small force.

We are able to go about our daily lives in peace today only because of our military and naval personnel who are on duty 24 hours a day, many under the sea in nuclear submarines, able to annihilate anyone who launches another Pearl Harbor against us. That is why none has been launched.

We have peace not because our politicians are so wise, or our diplomats so clever, or our journalists so glib. We have peace because of other young lives willingly disrupted by military duty for the sake of our safety—and willing to join those buried in this cemetery, if need be.

Once a year is not too often to remember them. And if we ever forget them and the things they stand for, we may not have very many more years as a free people living in peace.

COSMIC JUSTICE
AND HUMAN REALITY

SOME IDEAS ARE SO FAR-FETCHED that no one who actually thought about them could really believe them. But such ideas may be fiercely defended because they are the basis of other things that people do believe in.

"Equality" is one of the crucial far-fetched ideas of our time. From the soapbox demagogue to the highest court in the land, statistical disparities in outcomes have been treated as virtual proof that somebody was treated unfairly. Apparently there is no way that they could have performed differently, because of the implicit assumption of equality.

Yet most people would be hard-pressed to name two individuals who perform equally. What we usually mean when we rate two individuals equally is that they have offsetting advantages. But the same man is not even equal to himself on different days, much less at different periods of his life.

Anyone who has watched tennis matches, whether on the local playground or at Wimbledon, has seen player A come and out totally annihilate player B in the first set—and then turn around and lose the match. Not only equality but superiority is very unreliable.

What many people mean by equality is that the races, the sexes or other large groupings of people have no innate superiority over others. However, innate superiority, inferiority or equality are about how people are at the moment of conception. But nobody takes an I.Q. test at the moment of conception, nor do they apply for college or a job then.

By the time they do those things, a lot has happened—and it has seldom happen equally.

Even before the child is born, the mother's eating, drinking and smoking affect the formation of the little body inside, including the formation of the brain. The children of teenage mothers have lower I.Q.s, even when you take account of all sorts of social variables.

There are significant I.Q. differences between identical twins when one is born substantially heavier than the other. Apparently whatever has allowed one twin to gain more nutrition during their development leaves the other permanently a little behind mentally, long after they have grown up and their weights are the same.

Research has also shown that it makes a big difference whether a small child is constantly talked to and stimulated in various ways or is just laid down to vegetate somewhere, while the mother watches her soap operas or sleeps off a hangover. It is not just a matter of what information is conveyed to the child. Constant interaction, even with low-I.Q. adults, has been shown to improve a child's I.Q. It is not what they convey to him but what they stimulate in him.

The physical development of the brain itself is greater in children who have much interaction and many things to think about, however simple those things may be. In the crucial early years especially, you have to use it or lose it.

Painful as it is to think of all the individuals and groups who have lost golden opportunities because of these and numerous other differences beyond their control, the only thing worse than thinking about it is refusing to think about it. A grand pretense, endlessly repeated, does not become a hard fact.

The tendency to explain differences by either genetics or discrimination ignores very large differences that cannot be attributed to either. Numerous visitors to the antebellum South wrote, either privately or publicly, of the great differences between southern whites and northern whites. These differences ranged from church services to sex, from child-rearing to alcohol consumption, from entrepreneurship to violence. Yet whites in the two sections of the country were of the same race, language, religion and legal status.

Nevertheless, their differences extended across a broad spectrum, including the per capita rate of inventions patented, which was several times as high outside the South. Many 19th century writers, including de Tocqueville, attributed these differences to the concentration of slavery in the South. But the two groups of whites who settled in different regions of the United States came from different regions of Britain, where the same differences existed long before either of them had any slaves.

Slavery is not a magic answer to historic questions, either for whites or blacks. Only the prevailing refusal to acknowledge that some cultures are far more effective than others leads us to grasp desperately for such all-purpose explanations of performance differences, including genetics or discrimination.

FROM MARXISM TO THE MARKET

RECENTLY A STUDENT WROTE to ask me a familiar question: How and why had I changed from a young leftist to someone with my present views, which are essentially in favor of free markets and traditional values? In a sense, it was not so much a change in underlying philosophy as in my vision of how human beings operate.

Back in the days when I was a Marxist, my primary concern was that ordinary people deserved better and that elites were walking all over them. That is still my primary concern, but the passing decades have taught me that political elites and cultural elites are doing far more damage than the market elites could ever get away with doing.

For one thing, the elites of the marketplace have to compete against one another. If General Motors doesn't make the kind of car you want, you can always turn to Ford, Chrysler, Honda, Toyota and others. But if the Environmental Protection Agency goes off the deep end, there is no alternative agency doing the same thing that you can turn to instead.

Even when a particular corporation seems to have a monopoly of its product, as the Aluminum Company of American once did, it must compete with substitute products. If Alcoa had jacked up the price of aluminum to exploit its monopoly position, many things that were made of aluminum would have begun to be made of steel, plastic, and numerous other materials.

The net result of market forces was that, half a century after it became a monopoly, Alcoa was charging less for aluminum than it did at the beginning. That was not because the people who ran the company were nice. It was because market competition left them no viable alternative.

How you look at the free market depends on how you look at human beings. If everyone were sweetness and light, socialism would be the way to go. Within the traditional family, for example, resources are often lavished on children, who don't earn a dime of their own. It is domestic socialism and even the most hard-bitten capitalists practice it.

Maybe someday we will discover creatures in some other galaxy who can operate a whole society that way. But the history of human beings shows that a nation with millions of people cannot operate like one big family.

The rhetoric of socialism may be inspiring, but its actual record is dismal. Countries which for centuries exported food have suddenly found themselves forced to import food to stave off starvation, after agriculture was socialized. This has happened all over the world, among people of every race.

Anyone who saw the contrast between East Berlin and West Berlin, back in the days when half the city was controlled by the Communists, can have no doubts as to which system produces more economic benefits for ordinary people.

Even though the people in both parts of the city were of the same race, culture and history, those living under the Communists were painfully poorer, in addition to having less freedom. Much the same story could be told in Africa, where Ghana relied on socialistic programs and the Ivory Coast relied more on the marketplace, after both countries became independent back in the 1960s.

Ghana started off with all the advantages. Its per capita income was double that in the Ivory Coast. But, after a couple of decades under different economic systems, the bottom 20 percent of people in the Ivory Coast had higher incomes than 60 percent of the people in Ghana.

Halfway around the world, it was much the same story in Southeast Asia. Burma once had a higher per capita income than Thailand, until Burma went socialist. Today, Thailand's per capita income is 5 times that of Burma.

Economic inefficiency is by no means the worst aspect of socialistic government. Trying to reduce economic inequality by increasing political inequality, which is essentially what Marxism is all about, has cost the lives of millions of innocent people under Stalin, Mao, Pol Pot and others.

Politicians cannot be trusted with a monopoly of power over other people's lives. Thousands of years of history have demonstrated this again and again and yet again.

While my desires for a better life for ordinary people have not changed from the days of my youthful Marxism, experience has taught the bitter lesson that the way to get there is the opposite of what I once thought.

HOGWASH IS HAPPENING

"BOOK BANNING IS HAPPENING NOW!!"

That is what the sign said in the midst of a big display in the bookstore window. As it turned out, book banning was not happening. Hogwash was happening.

The books in the display were not banned. You can get them at bookstores from sea to shining sea. The government itself buys some of these books. Many of them are circulating in the tens of thousands, and some in the millions.

A poster in the display proclaimed this to be "Banned Books Week." The kind of shameless propaganda that has become commonplace in false charges of "censorship" or "book banning" has apparently now been institutionalized with a week of its own.

Someone called the 1930s a "low, dishonest decade." The 1990s are a serious competitor for that title. False charges of banning or censorship are so common that they are seldom challenged for evidence or even for a definition.

To call a book "banned" because someone decided that it was unsuitable for their particular students or clientele would be to make at least 99 percent of all books "banned." Few individuals or institutions can afford to buy even one percent of the vast number of books that are published annually. They must exercise judgment and that judgment is necessarily in the negative most of the time.

If we are not going to call every book that is not purchased by an institution "banned," then how will we define this nebulous but emotional word?

Usually some school or library officials decide to buy a particular book and then some parents or others object that it is either unsuitable for children or unsuitable in general, for any of a number of reasons. Then the cry of "censorship" goes up, even if the book is still being sold openly all over town.

If the criterion of censorship is that the objection comes from the general public, rather than from people who run schools and libraries, then that is saying that the parents and taxpayers have no right to a say about what is done with their own children or their own money.

This is a pretty raw assertion of pre-emptive superiority—and while many of the self-anointed may think this way, few are bold enough to come right out and say it. Fraudulent words like "censorship" and "banned" enable them to avoid having to say it upfront.

Some of the books shown seemed pretty innocuous to me—but there is no more reason why my opinion should prevail than the opinion of someone else, especially when that someone else is a parent or taxpayer. However, other books in the display were pure propaganda for avant-garde notions that are being foisted onto vulnerable and unsuspecting children in the name of "education."

Parents have not only a right but a duty to object when their children are being used as objects for other people's ideological crusades, especially when brainwashing replaces education in the public schools. Let the ideologues argue their ideas openly with adults in the marketplace of ideas, not take cowardly advantage of children behind their parents' backs.

There is no point arguing about whether this book or that book should or should not have been taken off the shelves. There would not be an issue in the first place if different people did not have different opinions on that point. The question is why some people's opinions are called "censorship" and other people's opinions are not.

No one calls it censorship when the old *McGuffey's Readers* are no longer purchased by the public schools (though they are still available and are actually being used in some private schools). No one calls it censorship if books by Rush Limbaugh are not put into libraries and schools in every town, hamlet and middlesex village.

It is only when the books approved by the elite intelligentsia are objected to by others that it is called censorship. Apparently we are not to talk back to our betters.

All this is just one more skirmish in the cultural wars of our time. In war, someone pointed out long ago, truth is the first casualty. Those who are spreading hysteria about book banning and censorship know that they are in a war, but too many of those who thought-lessly repeat their rhetoric do not.

It is not enough to see through fraudulent rhetoric in a particular case if you continue to listen gullibly to those who have used such rhetoric to muddy the waters.

There should have been a sign in that bookstore window saying "Hogwash is happening." That's what really rates two exclamation points—and perhaps a National Hogwash Week.

MAGIC NUMBERS

RECENT POLITICAL CONTROVERSIES over changing the consumer price index might leave the false impression that someone just goofed on this particular statistic, making it an inaccurate measure of inflation. The inaccuracy of the CPI is hard to deny, but this is to some extent inherent not only in this statistic, but in many other statistics on which we rely uncritically.

Hospitals and doctors, for example, are sometimes judged by the mortality rates of their patients. Commonsensical as this may sound, it violates one of the most elementary requirements for valid statistics: There is no comparable group of patients with whom these mortality rates can be compared.

Some of the best hospitals and some of the best doctors get the toughest cases. If they can save three-quarters of the cases on which others have given up, that is a major achievement, even if it leaves them with a 25 percent mortality rate.

The absence of comparable samples likewise completely undermines a recent study which "proved"—at least to the media's satisfaction—that spanking does no good and seems to do harm.

The study followed children who had been spanked and children who had not. After several months, it turned out that the spanked children's behavior was worse than that of the children who were not spanked.

What was lacking was a comparable group of children *with given behavior* at the outset, so that the effect of spanking could be isolated. Unless parents were spanking their children for no reason, chances are that those who got whacked on the backside were doing something to deserve it.

The lack of what statisticians call a "control group" to compare is just one of the reasons for meaningless and misleading statistics. Failure to define what you are talking about is another.

For example, when a man migrates from Italy to Australia and marries a women who is an Australian citizen, that is counted as an "intermarriage" in statistical studies. It may well be that her family knows his family because they both came from the same town in Italy but the difference in their citizenship status makes this just as much of an intermarriage on paper as if an Eskimo had married a Spaniard.

For years, Keynesian economists talked about the trade-off between inflation and unemployment, and how government should "fine tune" the economy to pick the best combination. In practice, it turned out that the government was lucky to get the right channel.

The source of this Keynesian optimism were a set of statistics known as the "Phillips Curve," which showed how inflation and unemployment were related to one another in the early postwar years. Alas for the Keynesians, statistics for later years showed no such correlation. We learned the hard way that we could end up with both high inflation and high unemployment—"stagflation"—and now we are having low rates of both.

Unfortunately, when numbers seem to support an existing belief, they are quick to be accepted, whether they involve spanking or unemployment.

Some people grasp at statistics the way a drowning man grasps at straws. Since you can always add numbers together and get a total, regardless of what the numbers are about, all sorts of statistical rankings are eagerly watched—when in fact what should be watched are the ways these numbers are put together.

For years, parents and students, as well as colleges and universities, have been watching the academic rankings published annually by *U.S. News & World Report.* Indeed, more than a few cases of fudging the facts have been discovered among academic administrators seeking to boost their rankings because of the importance attached to them.

Even if the statistics themselves were perfectly honest, however, they would prove practically nothing. When professors' salaries go into the statistical witches' brew, for example, this represents something that has very little to do with the actual teaching of students. In a survey by *The Chronicle of Higher Education,* only 13 percent of professors said that teaching is rewarded. Research, and especially research grants, are what affect the paycheck.

Recently, some academic institutions—including some ranked number one—have belatedly begun to challenge these rankings. Let's hope that this is the beginning of a trend.

THE MULTICULTURALISM CULT

THE WORLD HAS BEEN MULTICULTURAL for centuries before this word was coined. Moreover, it has been multicultural in a very real and practical way, directly the opposite of the way being urged by today's "multiculturalism" cult.

The very paper on which these words are written was invented in China, as was the art of printing. The letters come from ancient Rome and the numbers from India, via the Arabs. All this is being written by a man whose ancestors came from Africa, while listening to music by a Russian composer.

Even leaders of nations are not necessarily from those nations themselves. Napoleon was not French, Stalin was not Russian and Hitler was not German.

Crops have been as multicultural as people. Much of the world's rubber comes from Malaysia, but the Malaysian rubber trees themselves came from seeds brought from Brazil. The cocoa grown in Nigeria and the potatoes grown in Ireland likewise both originated in the Western Hemisphere before Columbus arrived.

A list of all the crops, technology and ideas that have spread from one people or one nation to another would be a list of most of the crops, technology or ideas in the world. The reason why all these things spread was, quite simply, that some things were considered better than others—and people wanted the best they could get.

This is completely the contrary to the philosophy of the "multiculturalism" cult, where things are not better or worse, but just different. Yet people around the world do not simply "celebrate diversity," they pick and choose which of their own cultural features they want to keep and which they want to dump in favor of something better from somebody else.

When Europeans first discovered paper and printing from China, they did not "celebrate diversity," they stopped giving themselves writers' cramp from copying scrolls and started letting the printing presses do the work. When American Indians saw horses for the first time after Europeans brought them here, they did not "celebrate diversity," they started riding off to hunt instead of walking.

Everything from automobiles to antibiotics has spread around the world because people wanted the best they could get, not the inefficient ways that the multiculturalist cult calls "living in harmony with nature." Too often, before modern medicine was accepted, that meant dying young instead of living to a healthy old age. People preferred to live, even if it wasn't "in harmony with nature."

The issue is not what I say or what the multiculturalists say. The issue is what millions of human beings actually do when they have a choice. Around the world, they treat cultural features as things that help them cope with life, not museum pieces to oooh and aaah over.

When they find their own ways of doing some things better, they keep them. When they find someone else's ways of doing other things better, they use them and drop what they used before. What they do not do is what the multiculturalists do—say that it is all just a matter of "perceptions," that nothing is better or worse than anything else.

Multiculturalism is one of those affectations that people can indulge in when they are enjoying all the fruits of modern technology and can grandly disdain the processes that produced them. None of this would be anything more than another of the many foibles of the human race, except that the cult of multiculturalism has become the new religion of our schools and colleges, contributing to the mushing of America. It has become part of the unexamined assumptions underlying public policy and even decisions in courts of law.

Who would be surprised that people from different cultural backgrounds are "represented" differently in different jobs, colleges, or income levels, except for the unspoken assumption that these different cultures are equally effective for all things?

Yet you need only turn on the television set and watch professional basketball to realize that one segment of the population plays the game a lot better than others. If you watch the commercials that sponsor these events, you are often watching ads for beer companies that were almost invariably established by people of German ancestry.

Since Germans have been brewing beer since the days of the Roman Empire, should we be surprised that they excel as much in this as blacks excel in basketball? Any standard based on quality will have "over-representation" and "under-representation" of different groups, however much such "disparate impact" may shock the editorial writers and provoke judges to rush in where angels fear to tread.

LITTLE THINGS

SOMETIMES LITTLE THINGS give you clues about big things.

The other day, I was practicing tennis at a local playground, with the aid of a machine that fires the ball over the net to me. A little boy whose father was practicing on the court next to me became fascinated with the machine.

The little fellow, about four or five years old, started walking over onto the court where I was playing—on the side of the net facing the machine.

"No, no," I said, "that's dangerous."

The little boy kept walking onto my court, facing into the machine, which was still firing tennis balls in various directions as it turned from side to side. His father said nothing.

"That's dangerous!" I repeated, as I put down my tennis racket and started toward the other side of the net to turn off the machine.

"Michael, why don't you come on back?" the father said.

"I'm going to have to leave," I said to his father, "because this is dangerous."

"No, we'll leave," the father said. "Come on, Michael."

"No!" Michael said, still staring with fascination into the machine as it continued turning and firing tennis balls.

"Oh, Michael, come on," his father pleaded—but still without making a move to go get him.

By this time, I had reached the machine and turned it off. Only then did Michael lose interest and leave with his father.

After this little experience with the modern middle-class parent in action (or inaction), I went home and read in the paper about a local teacher who had won a teaching award. Was this because her students had learned more than other students? Not at all.

Her greatest claim to fame was that she concentrated on giving her students "self-esteem." She didn't believe in a lot of academic demands, grading and homework. All that might have hurt the little darlings' self-esteem.

For all I know, Michael may have been one of her students. Certainly he was far less likely to have his self-esteem hurt by his father than to have a couple of teeth knocked out by a tennis ball shot out of a machine. If he got closer and was hit in the eye, he could have lost his sight in that eye.

On that evening's television news, one of the lead stories was about students at the University of Wisconsin rushing onto a football field, breaking down the barriers and injuring several of their fellow students in the crush. A police woman on the scene said that it was impossible to physically restrain a mob of that size when they get carried away.

Of course it is impossible to control everybody. That is why people used to teach their children self-control and obedience to rules and authorities. Today, that kind of talk only gets you a condescending smile, at best.

Our award-winning teacher had a sign on her classroom wall saying, "Question Authority." Today, there is barely enough authority around to question.

This mushy abdication of responsibility to instill discipline is not peculiar to the United States. Young British soccer fans have become notorious for crossing the channel and creating riots at international soccer matches on the continent.

About 1,500 years ago, barbarians from continental Europe invaded Britain and took over. Today, British soccer fans are getting their revenge.

While many civilizations have succumbed to the onslaughts of barbarian invaders, we may be the first to succumb to the onslaughts of barbarians growing up in our midst. Every child born into this world today is as uncivilized as the cave man. If nobody gets around to civilizing him, that is the way he will grow up.

All the lofty talk about the "root causes" of crime fail to notice the obvious: People commit crimes because they are people—because they are innately selfish and do not care how their behavior affects other people, unless they have been raised to behave otherwise or unless they fear the criminal justice system.

The same people who are undermining the notion of imposing either internal or external restraints on children have also been undermining the prosecution and punishment of criminals. They have succeeded all too well on both fronts.

We will all be paying the price of that success for a long time to come.

What is amazing is not that we bought some of these modern theories that became fashionable back in the 1960s. What is staggering is that we have not reconsidered after 30 years of watching the consequences.

WRONG TO KNOW?

NO RINGING PHRASE has been used more sweepingly—or more hypocritically—by the media than "the public's right to know." While journalists have repeatedly invoked this notion in defense of their own violations of individuals' privacy, public decency and the law, they have shown no such respect for this right when it comes to letting the public know things that go against political correctness.

Apparently it is wrong to know things that would upset the liberals' picture of the world—whether the particular issue involves abortion, Anita Hill, homosexuals or the homeless.

One of the things the public apparently has no right to know is what is meant by a "partial-birth abortion," despite the current controversy surrounding the issue. Nor is this something too complex for ordinary mortals to understand.

What is called a partial-birth abortion is causing a baby to be born feet first, leaving only his head just inside the mother's body.

Then he is deliberately killed by puncturing his head and sucking out the brains.

Keeping the head barely inside the mother's body serves no medical purpose. Instead, it serves the legal purpose of avoiding a charge of murder. Yet the media refuse to let the public know what actually happens in a partial-birth abortion—or "late-term abortion" as the politically correct prefer to call it—however much both broadcast and print journalists are willing to discuss oral sex and other things that the public has "a right to know."

Because of media concealment of the facts, liberals can get away with saying that this is a rare procedure and may be necessary to save the mother's life, along with other demonstrably false statements. The American Medical Association has condemned the procedure as medically unnecessary and recently one of those who had claimed that the procedure was rare confessed that he had lied.

When will the media confess to lying?

Perhaps the classic example of preventing the public from knowing things considered wrong to know was the media treatment of David Brock's book, *The Real Anita Hill,* when it was published a few years ago. The question is not whether one agrees or disagrees with what the book says. The question is whether the public should be allowed to know what the book says.

Whether in book reviews or in interviews with the author, the media's top priority seemed to be to prevent the book's central message from becoming known—namely, that there were numerous eyewitnesses who contradicted Anita Hill's sworn testimony on numerous points and who presented a picture of her chasing Clarence Thomas and complaining to them that he showed no interest in her beyond that of an employee. Other witnesses painted a picture of Anita Hill's character that belied her picture of shocked innocence and made her someone whose credibility was very questionable.

These witnesses ranged from F.B.I. agents to Professor Hill's own students and included at least one liberal Senator. Yet the public apparently had no "right to know" what Brock's book had said and to make up their own mind about the charges and counter-charges. Reviews and interviews repeatedly turned into attacks on Brock or on those who financed his research—anything to distract from the issues raised in his book or the evidence he presented.

While the media have repeatedly quoted a study suggesting that homosexuality is inborn, they have been strangely silent after the validity of that study has been called into question and the author investigated for possible misconduct in the way he arrived at his results. The public apparently has no "right to know" that the politically correct conclusions they keep hearing may not be factually correct.

Crimes committed by "the homeless" are also among the things that it seems to be wrong to know. These crimes, including vicious murders, are almost always attributed to someone described as "a drifter"—even though he might have been called one of "the homeless" before his foul deed caused him to be reclassified, in the interest of saving the image of those on the streets, towards whom the media wants us to feel generous or guilty.

Whatever one's views about abortion, Anita Hill, homosexuals, the homeless or a thousand other things, these views can be informed only if information is not suppressed by those whose business is to supply information rather than try to control public opinion through disinformation. If they insist on being propagandists instead of journalists, the public surely has a right to know that.

UNNATURAL RESOURCES

IT WAS JUST A PASSING PHRASE in a news story about the recent population conference in Cairo, but it said more than longer and more pretentious discussions: "Conference activists, many of whom are recipients of U. S. grants . . ." Inevitably, these activists ended up asking for billions more to be spent to stop "overpopulation."

Those billions will, of course, employ more people like themselves and give them both largess to dispense among their colleagues and power to wield over others. Government-funded efforts to get more government funding is the political equivalent of a perpetual motion machine. A steady drumbeat of alarms about "overpopulation," punctuated from time to time by headline-producing conferences, is one result.

How real is the danger that we are being constantly warned about?

The short answer is that the Malthusians have had nearly two centuries since Malthus first wrote about this supposed danger in 1798, and they have yet to show any correlation between population and poverty. There are, of course, densely populated poor countries like India, with 757 people per square mile, but there are also very prosperous countries like Japan with 814 people per square mile.

Then there are prosperous and thinly populated countries like the United States, with only 71 people per square mile—and desperately poor regions like sub-Saharan Africa with an average of 61 people per square mile.

As of any given time, both rich and poor countries are scattered across a wide spectrum of population densities. If this gives no support to overpopulation theories, history undermines those theories completely. Rising population and rising living standards have gone together ever since Malthus' time.

Those spreading population hysteria love to tell us how long it will take for the world's population to double. But they don't tell us what country's standard of living fell the last time its population doubled. Even among the supposedly most "overpopulated" countries, which one actually had a higher per capita income when their population was half of what it is today?

To those determined to believe in overpopulation theories, we have somehow just been lucky in having various methods of increasing the food supply come along—and our luck has got to run out sometime. Similarly, we have lucked out in discovering more natural resources when we needed them, but this luck too has to end, if we believe the Chicken Littles.

Both notions of "luck" assume away what is at issue: Was there any reason to believe the overpopulation theory in the first place? If not, then we need not make the further arbitrary assumption of "luck" in having escaped for the moment.

Malthus had no empirical data on which to base the famous geometrical ratios of population increase and arithmetic ratio of food growth which he unveiled in 1798. Like Marx, he had the gift of dramatic imagery, cataclysmic prophecy and an air of "science." It seems almost mean-spirited to expect him to have had his facts straight too.

Later editions of Matlhus' *Essay on the Principle of Population* had lots of numbers, but these were used as illustrations of a vision, not as empirical tests of an hypothesis. As the late Nobel Prize-winning economist George Stigler put it: "Malthus simply had no canons of evidence." Neither do his latter-day followers.

The role of statistics remains that of illustrating a presupposition. These statistics show, for example, how long it takes population to double, or what will happen if you extrapolate any trend to infinity— almost invariably disaster.

Every evening, the temperature begins falling after sundown. Extrapolate that trend and the numbers will "prove" that we will all be frozen solid before the week is out. But numbers do not live lives of their own. They are generated by some process, and until you understand that process, the numbers mean nothing.

The same spinning of the earth which took us out of the sunlight in the evening will bring us back into the sunlight the next morning, and temperatures will begin to rise again. It is not a matter of escaping disaster by "luck."

Economic processes likewise signal through prices the costs of raising children and the costs of using natural resources. Moreover, contrary to the vision of the anointed, other people are not oblivious to their options or the costs of those options.

Contrary to hysteria about the exhaustion of natural resources, the known reserves of petroleum, for example, are greater than they were a quarter of a century ago, and the prices of many other natural resources have been falling as a result of their abundance.

That is good news for most of us but it is bad news for those trying every avenue by which they may impose their superior wisdom and virtue on others. Look for more international conferences, financed by the unnatural resources of government.

LOVE IS A FOUR-LETTER WORD

LOVE IS A FOUR-LETTER WORD, but you don't hear it nearly as often as you hear some other four-letter words. It may be a sign of our times that everyone seems to be talking openly about sex, but we seem to be embarrassed to talk about love.

Sex alone will not even reproduce the human race, because babies cannot survive the first week of life without incredible amounts of care. That care comes from love. If the parents are too wretched to give the infant the attention he needs, then a general love of babies must lead others to set up some backup system, so that the child does not die of neglect.

The shallow people who have turned our schools into propaganda centers for the counterculture try hard to take love out of human relations. Between men and women, for example, there is just sex, if you believe the clever anointed.

But why should we believe them? Why have there been such painful laments—in letters, literature, poetry and song—for so many centuries about the breakup of love affairs? Because there are no other members of the opposite sex available? Not at all.

Sex is almost always available, if only commercially. But love is a lot harder to find. Some people do not even try after their loved one is gone. Some give up on life itself.

In short, what millions of people have done for hundreds of years gives the lie to the self-important cynics who want to reduce everything to an animal level.

Actually, many animals behave in ways which suggest that love is important to them as well, not only among their own species but also with human beings. Stories of dogs who have rescued or defended their owners, even at the cost of their lives, go back for centuries.

Why is love so out of fashion with the intelligentsia and others who are striving to be "with it"?

Love is one of those bonds which enable people to function and societies to flourish—without being directed from above. Love is one of the many ways we influence each other and work out our interrelated lives without the help of the anointed. Like morality, loyalty, honesty, respect, and other immaterial things, love is one of the intangibles without which the tangibles won't work.

Intellectuals are not comfortable with that. They want to be able to reduce everything to something material, predictable and—above all—controllable. Many want to be in charge of our lives, not have us work things out among ourselves, whether through emotional ties or the interactions of the marketplace.

Another four-letter word that has fallen out of favor is "duty." It has not been banned. It has just been buried under tons of discussions of "rights." The two words used to be linked, but not any more.

In the real world, however, rights and duties are as closely tied as ever. If *A* has a right to something, then *B* has a duty to see that he gets it. Otherwise *A* has no such right.

When it is a right to freedom of speech, then it is the duty of judges to stop the government from shutting him up—or to let him sue if they do. The big problem comes when it is no longer a question of rights to be left alone but rights to things that other people have to produce. When it is a right to "decent housing," for example, that means other people have a duty to produce that housing and supply it to you—whether or not you are willing to pay what it costs.

Only because the inherent link between rights and duties is broken verbally are advocates for all sorts of sweeping new rights able to sidestep the question as to why someone else must provide individuals with what they are unwilling to provide for themselves.

The claim is often made or implied that people may be willing to provide for themselves but are simply unable to do so. But, when push comes to shove, many of the intelligentsia will admit that it doesn't matter to them why someone doesn't have something that he needs. He has a "right" to it. It also doesn't matter how someone caught AIDS, he has no duty to avoid it but others have a duty to pay for it.

What is involved is not just some words but a whole vision of life. If one has the vision of the anointed who want to control other people's lives, then all those things which enable us to function independently of them and of government programs are suspect.

Four-letter words like love, duty, work, and save are hallmarks of people with a very different vision, who make their own way through life without being part of some grandiose scheme of the anointed or of government bureaucracies that administer such schemes. No wonder those words are not nearly as popular as other four-letter words.

THE MUSHING OF AMERICA

THE ENVIRONMENTALISTS CELEBRATED "the greening of America" but there is another trend which is even more pervasive—and which is nothing to celebrate: the mushing of America.

Prosecutors, who see obviously guilty defendants either acquitted or let off with convictions for much lesser crimes than the ones they committed, complain that juries are too easily swayed by emotional appeals based on unsubstantiated claims of unhappy childhoods. Professors complain that today's college students have many passionate opinions but very little ability to use logic to support those opinions or to analyze opposing views. In the media, buzzwords increasingly replace thought and non sequiturs have become so common as to cause no notice or embarrassment.

What logicians call "the fallacy of composition" has come into its own. The notion that what is true of a part is true of the whole is the lifeblood of TV programs like Oprah and Donahue, where great issues of public policy are reduced to how particular individuals feel. For example, when someone said that our government should not ransom hostages being held in the Middle East, Donahue's reply was: "But suppose it was your brother they were holding?"

In a similar vein, *New York Times* columnist Anna Quindlen replied to those who objected to disruptions by AIDS activists by saying: "If I could help give someone I loved a second chance, or even an extra year of life, what people think would not worry me a bit." In other words, if it helps *A*, who cares what it does to *B*, *C*. *D*, and the others—or to law and order in a society where mob rule becomes the way to get what you want?

Another pervasive—and dangerous—sign of the mushy thinking of our time are the flagrantly fraudulent phrases that pass muster in the media and in politics. None is more fraudulent that the word "asking" in discussions of public policy issues.

Liberals love to say things like, "We're just asking everyone to pay their fair share." But government is not about asking. It is about *telling*. The difference is fundamental. It is the difference between making love and being raped, between working for a living and being a slave.

The Internal Revenue Service is not asking anybody to do anything. It confiscates your assets and puts you behind bars if you don't pay.

When parents objected to having their children exposed to other children with AIDS in the public schools, Anna Quindlen said that we should "ask some parents to put their children at some risk, however small, for the sake of principle and fairness."

But the schools were not asking the parents anything. They were *telling* them that their children must be subjected to risk—and that it was none of the parents' business to know who or where the carriers of this fatal disease were.

To challenge the buzzwords of the hour by demanding evidence is to betray your age—and your recalcitrance in the face of attempts to raise your consciousness. When the buzzword "diversity" is used, all brain cells are supposed to stop functioning, so that a rosy glow of feeling can take over.

Nothing is more rigidly conformist than "diversity." Use the generic "he" and it proves that you despise women. Fail to keep up with the ever-changing names for various racial and ethnic groups, and it proves you are a racist. In an age when four-letter words come easily to people's lips, you cannot use the four-letter word "work" without offending the homeless or a word like "quota" without betraying depths of malign intentions to all sorts of groups.

Neither logic nor evidence is considered an acceptable excuse for violating the taboos against questioning the sacred buzzwords. To ask whether all individuals who are less successful (the "disadvantaged") were handicapped from the outset or just failed to take advantage of their opportunities is to risk being classified as "judgmental," at best.

The very fact that exercising judgment now has negative connotations is one of the many symptoms of the mushing of America.

The more or less spontaneous mushy thinking that comes from laziness has long since been supplemented by systematic indoctrination in mushiness in our public schools and even in many colleges and universities. Issues are presented in terms of how you "feel" about this or that situation, not what structures of logic or what reservoirs of information are necessary for dealing with it responsibly. Students are being asked to play-act as if they were in Congress or in the White House responding to a crisis—as so many in those institutions also seem to be play-acting.

Repeated studies that show how little our high school graduates—or even Ivy League college graduates—know about basic things reflect how little such knowledge is considered necessary.

Mush is self-reinforcing. As fewer and fewer people are trained to analyze, those who do can be considered mere oddballs and both our personal and our national decisions can increasingly be made on the basis of mush.

ORPHANS AND ORPHANAGES

ORPHANS AND ORPHANAGES have been in the news recently on both sides of the Atlantic. Western couples on their way to Russia to adopt Russian orphans have suddenly been told that a new policy puts these adoptions on hold. No one knows when—if ever—they will be allowed to adopt the children they were once told were now ready for them to take into their homes.

Russian nationalists do not like having Americans or other Europeans adopting their children. Children's opportunities for a normal home and family are being sacrificed to the embarrassments and resentments of adults.

It has long been the same story in the United States, where minority social workers and politicians have not only prevented white couples from adopting minority children, but have even devastated these children's lives by ripping them away from white foster parents who are often the only parents they have ever known.

Using children as political footballs is even uglier than most of the ugly things that happen in politics. After House Speaker-elect Newt Gingrich's discussions of welfare reform options, so many politicians and editorial writers have seized upon the word "orphanage" to make political hay that there is little hope of a rational public discussion of the very serious issues involved in our present welfare tragedy.

At the heart of that tragedy is children having children. Babies born to teenage girls, whether black or white, have lower birth weights, lower IQs, and a greater chance of being premature or of dying in infancy. These children are also more likely to be neglected or abused, and in later life to become problems or disasters to those around them.

It would be utopian to think that there is some easy way out of all this, with no one getting hurt. Plenty of people are being hurt badly as things stand now. The big question is: Which way will the pain be worse?

Unfortunately, the media's love of dramatizing individual sob stories may make it impossible to make a rational choice. If a successful policy that the media pundits don't like produces only seven people who are worse off, each of those seven people will be featured on television news every night for a week—and presented as if they were typical.

As long as irresponsible teenage girls get an automatic subsidy for having babies, there is little hope of changing the basic pattern. Nor can we realistically expect any of the social miracles that are so freely promised by those who think that government programs can produce "parenting skills." The very phrase itself is an evasion of the bitter reality that attitudes are the problem, not "skills."

In the liberals' world of "virtual reality," all problems are caused by things beyond the individual's control—and can be solved by having government come to the rescue with the taxpayer's money and the social programs of the anointed. When mothers are too ir-responsible to get their children vaccinated, this becomes trans-formed into a question of cost, of "access," of anything other than what it is.

How do you ensure that children get taken care of without giv-ing their mothers a free ride? There are any number of possibilities that could be explored, with orphanages being a last resort for the worst cases.

Nobody believes that an orphanage is better than a normal home. But we have to make our choices among the alternatives actually available—and some of those alternatives are pretty hideous. In some cases, a normal home is nowhere on the horizon and an or-phanage may be the best of a bad set of options.

It is either silly or dishonest to compare the cost of caring for a child in an orphanage with the cost of a year of college, as some clever people are doing. That same ridiculous comparison has been made as regards the cost of keeping someone in prison. But these are not the alternatives.

The real alternative may be to leave a child to be abused by a rotten mother and to grow up to become a lifelong parasite or crimi-nal. It is worth paying a lot to avoid that.

Hillary Clinton's claim that proposed welfare reforms would mean putting children in orphanages because their mothers cannot find jobs is more of the liberals' virtual reality. Nobody advocates any such thing and it is truly stretching the imagination to conjure up a picture of alcoholic, abusive and irresponsible girls trudging bravely from employer to employer, looking in vain for work.

Nobody wants children to suffer. The only question is which way they will suffer more. That is a tough question and finding some vi-able answers will require some very careful study, soul-searching and hard choices.

Virtual reality, political cheap shots and individual sob stories are not going to help.

REVISIONISTS AGAINST AMERICA

AN AMERICAN OF CHINESE ANCESTRY got into big trouble when the private school at which he was teaching had a public discussion of the American bombing of Hiroshima. He recalled how, as someone growing up in China, he had rejoiced when he heard of the bombing, knowing that it could deliver his people from the horrors inflicted on them by the Japanese.

That of course was not the politically correct response, as he soon discovered from the backlash, hostility and ostracism that eventually culminated in his leaving the school. The anointed do not want anyone upsetting their vision. When they say "diversity," this is not what they have in mind.

Hiroshima has become one of many symbols of a countercultural hostility to America among the intelligentsia in general and the "revisionist" historians in particular. The 50th anniversary of the bombing of Hiroshima on August 6, 1945 galvanized *Newsweek* magazine into Monday-morning-quarterbacking, half a century after that Sunday.

The revisionist line is that it was unnecessary to bomb Hiroshima. We could have invaded, we could have negotiated a settlement, we could have done all sorts of things.

Newsweek magazine's estimate today is that there might have been 20,000 Americans killed in an invasion of Japan. This is quite a contrast with the estimates of the people who had the heavy responsibility of fighting the war at the time.

General Douglas MacArthur, who had been selected to command the invasion of Japan, before the atomic bomb was tested and shown to work, told Secretary of War Stimson to expect more than a million American casualties alone. British Prime Minister Winston Churchill also expected more than a million American casualties, together with half a million casualties among the British troops who were scheduled to hit the beaches with the Americans.

Anyone familiar with the history of the Japanese soldiers' bitter resistance to the death—very few were captured alive—will have no trouble understanding why such huge casualties were expected. American marines lost more than 5,000 men taking the little island of Iwo Jima and the Japanese themselves suffered more than 100,000 deaths when Americans captured Japan's outlying island of Okinawa. That was more than were killed at Hiroshima or Nagasaki.

Newsweek's pushover scenario, which would have had Japan defeated in 90 days, would be funny if it were not so sick. Winston Churchill's estimate to the House of Commons would have had the war with Japan ending in 1946 and the Pentagon's estimate was that Japan might even hold out until 1947.

Not only was there a Japanese army which had proven its toughness and skill on many a battlefield, there were 5,000 kamikaze planes ready for suicide attacks on Americans invading their homeland. If these planes managed to take out just 5 Americans each, they alone would have killed more troops than those in *Newsweek's* rosy scenario.

Japan's civilian population, including children, were also being mobilized and trained in suicide attacks on enemy troops and tanks. It would have been one of the great bloodbaths of all time.

Of course Japan could have been defeated without the atomic bomb. But at what cost in lives of people killed in other ways and in larger numbers?

The other tack taken by the revisionist historians is to say that Japan was "ready to surrender" before the atomic bombs were dropped. The most obvious question is: Why didn't they do it, then? Indeed, why didn't they do it after Hiroshima was bombed, and thereby spare Nagasaki?

Whatever negotiations may have been going on behind the scenes, surrender was by no means a done deal. Even after both cities had been destroyed, it took the unprecedented intervention of the emperor himself to get the military men to agree to surrender. And even as the emperor's message was being broadcast, some military officers were killed trying to storm the studio where the broadcast originated.

The real question is not whether Japan was willing to negotiate some kind of end to the war but whether it was ready to accept the terms being offered, which involved not merely military capitulation but acceptance of American occupation of their homeland. It was this occupation, like the occupation of Germany, which turned a militaristic nation that had launched several wars in recent times into a peaceful and democratic country.

This was an historic achievement, made possible by the terms of surrender—which in turn were made possible by the two atomic bombs. On net balance, this saved not only American and British lives, but even Japanese lives—not to mention the lives of people in Asia like our Chinese American school teacher who told a bitter truth which the anointed did not want to hear.

"PUBLIC SERVICE"— OR DISSERVICE?

ACCORDING TO ONE OF THE COLLEGE GUIDES, students taking English 6 at Amherst "must volunteer" to tutor in a local high school. Orwellian Newspeak has become so common in academia that apparently no one sees the irony in the notion that a student "must volunteer."

Trendy colleges and high schools across the country are requiring "service" to "the community" as ways of earning academic credit or even as a precondition for receiving a diploma. In Washington, "national service" is now in vogue—another "feel good" idea financed with other people's money.

What is truly frightening is the casual ease with which so many people believe that they can define what is and is not a "service" to the society.

Stanford University's law school, for example, sends students and others over to the nearby ghetto in East Palo Alto to fight against the expulsion of hoodlums from the public school system there. It would be hard to imagine a greater disservice to the black community than allowing their children's education to be disrupted, undermined or destroyed by trouble-makers, thugs and young drug dealers who want to remain classified as "students" only so that they can remain on campus and sell crack.

We all know what road is paved with good intentions. Whether students working in a soup kitchen or a homeless shelter or doing any of the other "services" being performed for academic credit are in fact making society better or worse, on net balance, is an open question, not a foregone conclusion.

When weighing the immediate benefits against the promotion of dependency and the enlargement of an army of idle people on the streets, creating more than their share of mischief and crime, the net balance is at least debatable.

But, even if we assume that every "service" performed by students is in fact a service, that still leaves the very large question as to why it should be performed by students.

No doubt rescuing people from burning buildings would be a service, but do we want students to do it—or is this something we want left to professionally-trained fire departments? Even where students have the necessary skills, is there no value to their time in doing what they are in schools and colleges to do—namely to develop their minds in preparation for a lifetime of contributing to society in a wide variety of ways?

Why are parents making financial sacrifices to send their children to colleges and universities, if the time they spend there is of so little value that it can be used to perform the chores of amateur social workers? Does an academic institution have so little dedication to its own mission that it must seek tangential activities to justify its existence?

Much that is done in the name of "service" not only fails to advance the development of thinking skills but positively hinders it by substituting emotionally indelible but superficial experiences.

To call such activities an experience in "real life" is fraudulent, because real life is not pre-arranged for you by academic institutions. Nothing is more misleading than such phony "realism."

Like so much that is done under cover of academic pieties, "service" to others is all too often a means of propagandizing the students themselves with "politically correct" ideologies, getting them to feel sorry for those supposedly neglected or abused by society, and to see handouts and social engineering as the solution to social problems.

It can hardly be coincidental that those pushing hardest for "service" requirements in schools and colleges are so often also those pushing for the "politically correct" agenda of the left in general. This is a cheap way of insinuating their ideologies into inexperienced and vulnerable young minds, without having to make a real case in an open way that could be challenged by others.

Like so much else that is done by those who treat education as the continuation of politics by other means, the lasting damage that is done is not by insinuating a particular ideology, for people's ideologies change over time, regardless of what they were taught. The lasting damage is done to the development of critical thinking.

Learning to think, and to know what you are talking about, is a full-time occupation. Nowhere is this more true than in the formative years. Even naturally bright people can turn out to be nothing more than clever mush heads if the discipline of logic and the analytical dissection of many-sided empirical evidence is slighted for the sake of emotional "experiences."

Defining "service" and assigning it to others may be a big ego trip for some educators, but only to the extent that they are willing to sacrifice or prostitute education itself.

LATE-TALKING CHILDREN AND QUICK-LABELLING ADULTS

MARY'S SON JOHN WAS LATE IN WALKING and late in talking. Moreover, his mother said that he "drooled so that it looked as if I had poured water on the front of his shirt." Whatever anxieties she had about him were amplified by friends and relatives who warned her that she might someday have to have him "put away." Carol's son Kevin was also late in talking and was still wearing diapers when he was 4 years old. Annette's son Colin was 3 years and 9 months old to the day before he could say his own name—and he said very little else.

I learned about these and other late-talking children after I wrote a newspaper column about my son, who was nearly four years old before he could talk and who was also diagnosed as "physically uncoordinated" at school. But today, he and these other late-talking boys are now grown men and leading normal lives.

My son has a degree in computer science and, despite being labelled uncoordinated, he bowled his first 200 game while still a teenager. Since then, his highest bowling score has been 289. Perhaps if he were coordinated, he would have gotten the other 11 pins needed for a perfect game.

Late-talking is not something to take lightly. Often it is part of a whole collection of serious problems. But falsely labelling children is also a very serious problem—and sometimes a needless and devastating blow to parents already struggling to deal with their children as they are on a day-to-day basis, while living under a cloud of fear for their future.

Even more lasting damage can be done to the child, who is shunted aside into one of the many programs for children with "developmental disorders," "handicaps" or "autism." Whatever the potential of these children—and some turn out to be very bright—that potential is unlikely to be realized in settings like these.

While there have been innumerable studies of late-talking children in general, there is remarkably little attention paid to children who talk late but who otherwise have normal or above-normal intelligence. Experts consulted by their parents typically have little or nothing to offer as either explanation or advice—and even that little often turns out later to be completely wrong.

An informal group that formed as a result of writing to me about their late-talking children now consists of 33 sets of parents, representing 34 children because of twin girls in one family. They are the only girls among the children in the group.

A questionnaire I sent out to the group was filled in and returned by 17 sets of parents. The results were remarkable.

While the group is geographically and ethnically diverse, the children in it have very definite patterns. In addition to being 94 percent male, more than 60 percent of the children whose parents returned questionnaires had a close relative who was an engineer—and among the others, all had a relative who worked in chemistry, computers, accounting or some other analytical field. This leaves out one boy who was adopted and whose biological family history is unknown.

In addition to the children in the group, I have met several other late-talkers. All of them are male. Among those whose occupations or parents' occupations I know, all are working in some analytical field involving mathematics, science, computers or the like. The most famous late-talker of all was of course Albert Einstein.

Most late-talking children are not like this. But there is this minority with a very pronounced pattern.

There are other features to the pattern. More than 60 percent of these children had close relatives who played a musical instrument, some professionally.

Most of the children themselves also showed either analytical or musical talents early on, even while they were not talking. Some who were given non-verbal mental tests, such as putting puzzles together, often showed ability far ahead of other children their age.

One 3-year-old boy in our group has learned to use a computer and likes to play computer games. He knows which programs are in Windows, which are in DOS and how to get access to both.

While all this suggests heredity, such patterns are not found among all members of these families. None of the late-talking children in our group had a brother or sister who talked late, except of course for the twin girls. This also makes it doubtful whether the children are talking late because of the way their parents raised them.

While this is a predominantly male pattern, I have also learned of a girl who talked late in a small town in New Hampshire, though she is not part of our group. She graduated 13th in her high school class of more than 700—and is planning to major in engineering in college. Her father is an engineer.

Not all stories of late-talking children have happy endings, by any means. Even within our special group, one boy has been found to have severe hearing loss, so his talking late may be due to entirely different reasons from the others. Another boy is apparently autistic.

Some other children in the group were initially diagnosed as autistic and the diagnosis later changed. Sometimes an unqualified person said that the child was autistic and a specialist determined that he was not. At other times, the specialist reversed his own earlier diagnosis, after the child's later progress made it clear that he was not autistic.

What does all this mean? At the very least, it means that we should not be so quick to label young children. To me this also means that these special kinds of children should be researched by someone trained in such things—both for the children's sake and for the sake of a society which needs the talents they have, which can wither away if they are sidetracked into a blind alley of programs for retarded children.

FRAUD IN PHILLY

THE VOLUNTEERISM "SUMMIT" IN PHILADELPHIA may be a litmus test of whether we are still capable of thinking, or have been so well-conditioned to certain kinds of rhetoric that we respond as automatically as Pavlov's dog.

Consider the cry that what our social problems need are "one million more Americans" to volunteer. Currently an estimated 93 million Americans are volunteering. Why will 94 million be able to accomplish what 93 million clearly have not accomplished?

Consider the great symbolic act with which this summit began—the president and vice-president cleaning graffiti off the walls of a run-down neighborhood in Philadelphia. What message does that send: When you foul your own nest, we will come in and clean it up for you?

Worse yet, the hard-working, decent and law-abiding majority of Americans are made to feel guilty because others do not choose to work, to be decent or even to obey the law. Those who produce the things we all live on are supposed to "give something back" to those who produce nothing, and from whom nothing could have been taken.

When government or private officials with the welfare-state mentality enter poor neighborhoods, their concern and largess are disproportionately aimed at the trouble-makers and the irresponsible. What about those people in poor neighborhoods who are trying to do the right thing, who are trying to raise their children to be honest, self-reliant people, and to shelter them from the violence, the drugs and the moral squalor?

Too often such people are left feeling like chumps for not getting in on the goodies that are being handed out to those who know how to game the system.

Volunteerism cannot be assessed in the broad, sweeping terms of political rhetoric. There is no question that Red Cross volunteers in disaster areas, or people who visit invalids who have no one else to look after them, are performing a real service. But massive and indiscriminate welfare-statism has a track record of disaster, and privatizing it is not likely to change that.

If it were just a question of private philanthropy taking on the very same tasks once performed by government, before the era of budget retrenchment, then all that would be involved would be a matter of bookkeeping as to where the very same total expenses would show up. Any hope of change for the better depends on a net reduction of counterproductive behavior—which must begin by recognizing it as counterproductive, not by covering it up with non-judgmental euphemisms or by blaming "society."

The Philadelphia "summit" was primarily an opportunity for various political and media figures to showcase themselves by using pious rhetoric and symbolic gestures. For no one was that more true than for the chairman of this operation, General Colin Powell.

If anything good comes out of this media extravaganza, it may be the continuing exposures of General Powell's willingness to go along with the fundamental assumptions of the welfare state, while proclaiming himself a Republican and being proclaimed as a Republican presidential prospect.

If the Republicans think that what they need in the next presidential election is another George Bush or Bob Dole with a deeper tan, then Colin Powell is the man to lead them to the oblivion they will richly deserve.

Like Ross Perot, General Powell had a golden opportunity to unite and lead Americans out of the mess that politicians had gotten us into. Both, however, failed by confusing leading with pandering to popular illusions, and by confusing catch phrases with thought.

Colin Powell's life, especially, has been a contradiction to the welfare-statism and affirmative-action he has embraced far more since becoming a political prospect than he did in his best-selling autobiography. His gratuitous remarks on Tiger Woods' unwillingness to be racially pigeon-holed reflect no credit on Powell or on his ability to resist the dogmas of the race hustlers.

What the volunteerism summit has done, more than anything else, is to put on display the hollowness of contemporary rhetoric and the hollowness of so many of our "leaders." The great question now is how many Americans will see through all this and how many will be either taken in or intimidated into silence.

P. T. Barnum said that there is a sucker born every minute, but maybe the rate has speeded up in recent years.

PART II
THE ECONOMIC SCENE

"AFFORDABILITY"

MANY OF THE CANT WORDS OF POLITICS are simply evasions of reality. A prime example is the notion of making housing, college, health insurance, or other things "affordable."

Virtually anything can be made more affordable in isolation, simply by transferring resources to it from elsewhere in the economy, and having most of the costs absorbed by U. S. Treasury.

The federal government could make a Rolls Royce affordable for every American, but we would not be a richer country as a result. We would in fact be a much poorer country, because of all the vast resources transferred from other economic activities to subsidize an extravagant luxury.

Of course it might be nice to be sitting at the wheel of a Rolls Royce, but we might be sitting there in rags and tatters, and gaunt with hunger, after having squandered enormous amounts of labor, capital, and costly materials that could have been put to better use elsewhere. That doesn't happen in a market economy because most of us take one look at the price tag on a Rolls Royce and decide that it is time for another Toyota.

The very notion of making things affordable misses the key point of a market economy. An economy exists to make trade-offs, and a market economy makes the terms of those trade-offs plain with price tags representing the relative costs of producing different things. To have politicians arbitrarily change the price tags, so that prices no longer represent the real costs, is to defeat the whole purpose.

Reality doesn't change when the government changes price tags. The Clinton administration's talk about "bringing down health care costs" is not aimed at the costly legal environment in which medical science operates, or other sources of needless medical costs. It is aimed at price control, which hides costs rather than reducing them.

Hidden costs continue to take their toll—and it is often a higher toll than when these costs are freely transmitted through the marketplace. Less supply, poorer quality, and longer waits have been the consequences of price controls for all sorts of goods and services, in all sorts of societies, and for thousands of years of human history.

Why would anyone think that price controls on medical care would be any different, except for being more deadly in their consequences?

One of the political excuses for making things affordable is that a particular product or service is a "right." But this is only explaining one question-begging word with another.

Although Bill Clinton proclaimed at the Democratic convention in 1992 that "health care is a right, not a privilege," this neat dichotomy ignores the vast territory in between, where most decisions are made as trade-offs.

If health insurance is a right and not a privilege—and not even a subject of incremental trade-offs—then the same should be even more true of food. History in fact shows all too many instances of governments trying to keep food affordable, usually with disastrous consequences.

Whether in France during the 1790s, the Soviet Union after the Bolshevik revolution, or in newly independent African nations during the past generation, governments have imposed artificially low prices on food. In each case, this led to artificially low supplies of food and artificially high levels of hunger.

People who complain about the "prohibitive" cost of housing, or of going to college, for example, fail to understand that the whole point of prices is to be prohibitive.

Why do we go through this whole rigmarole of passing around dollar bills and writing each other checks, except to force everyone to economize on the country's inherently limited resources?

What about "basic necessities"? Shouldn't they be a "right"?

The idea certainly sounds nice. But the very fact that we can seriously entertain such a notion, as if we were God on the first day of creation, instead of mortals constrained by the universe we find in place, shows the utter unreality of failing to understand that we can only make choices among alternatives actually available.

For society as a whole, nothing comes as a "right" to which we are "entitled." Even bare subsistence has to be produced—and produced at a cost of heavy toil for much of human history.

The only way anyone can have a right to something that has to be produced is to force someone else to produce it for him. The more things are provided as rights, the less the recipients have to work and the more others have to carry their load.

That does not mean more goods are available than under ordinary market production, but less. To believe otherwise is to commit the Rolls Royce fallacy on a more mundane level.

For the government to make some things more affordable is to make other things less affordable—and to destroy people's freedom to make their own trade-offs as they see fit, in the light of economic realities, rather than political visions.

Trade-offs remain inescapable, whether they are made through a market or through politics. The difference is that price tags present all the trade-offs simultaneously, while political "affordability" policies arbitrarily fix on whatever is hot at the moment. That is why cities have been financing all kinds of boondoggles for years, while their bridges rusted and their roadways crumbled.

THE SOCIAL SECURITY PYRAMID

A RECENT LETTER FROM AN ELDERLY LADY living on Social Security reacts to a growing impression that people like her are "a drag on society" and closed: "We don't ask to live this long."

Perhaps the time is long overdue for those of us who have been criticizing the Social Security system to say, loud and clear: The elderly are not the villains. The politicians who set up this system have been guilty of a hoax from day one—and they have added more hoaxes as the years went by. That is why Social Security is either going to run out of money or else have to raise huge taxes from the younger workers, if the system is not changed in some fundamental way.

The first hoax, from which so many others flowed, was that Social Security was "insurance." Social Security has never been insurance. Any insurance company that set up a system like Social Security would be declared bankrupt and its officials would be jailed for fraud.

Insurance is based on taking the money of many people and investing it in something that will produce wealth that can later be used to pay off the claims of those people. With insurance, it does not matter how many old people and how many young people are involved, because the company is supposed to have enough assets to cover its liabilities—that is, what it has promised to pay out.

Social Security has never had enough assets to cover its liabilities. It is not insurance but a pyramid scheme, in which those who come in first get money from those who come in later. Like other pyramid schemes, there is always the great danger that those who come in later will be left holding the bag when the pyramid collapses. That is why such schemes are illegal—except when the government does it.

The puzzle is not why Social Security is in trouble now, but how it managed to escape collapse for so long. The big factor was that there was a small generation born in the 1930s, when Social Security began and larger generations born in the 1940s and 1950s. It was an expanding pyramid, which can pay off big for those who got in first.

Eventually, as the birthrate declined, there was no longer a very large younger generation supporting a much smaller older generation. Now, as the huge "baby boomer" generation begins to move toward retirement age, the big question is what will be left in the till for Social Security to pay to them.

The quick answer is not enough to cover what they have been promised, unless the Social Security taxes on the next generation soar to new heights, taking a third or more of their total income.

None of this is the fault of the elderly. Many older people point out that, if they had been allowed to take the same money that they put into Social Security and invest it in the stock market, for example, they would be getting more income than they receive from the government—and it wouldn't be costing the younger generation a thing.

How is this possible? Because real investments create more real wealth—more factories, homes, computers, etc.—which means that everyone can be better off at the same time. But money paid into Social Security is just more money for politicians to play around with. It is used to pay for everything from Congressional junkets and other federal boondoggles to making the national debt look smaller than it is on paper.

In other words, when you spend the money as fast as it comes into Washington, you don't build up any wealth for the future. Of course the Social Security system gets government bonds in exchange for the money that is spent, but this is just a paper transaction that represents no actual increase of real wealth. Government bonds represent nothing more than claims against future taxes.

When those claims start coming due big time, in the decades ahead, there is going to be hell to pay if the system continues as it is. Somebody is going to have to be defrauded, whether the old or the young—probably both, to one degree or another, through one trick or another.

The government can welsh on its promise to the elderly by delaying the age at which it begins to pay off, give them what they are entitled to with one hand and tax part of it back with the other or no doubt do other tricks that will surely occur to the clever folks in Washington. At the same time, they can think up new ways to drain money out of the paychecks of the young.

The only way out is to actually create more wealth, by allowing working people to invest their retirement money in something besides politicians' promises.

GIVING BUSINESS THE
BUSINESS

TELEVISION CHARACTERS LIKE J. R. EWING IN "DALLAS" may have portrayed businessmen as Machiavellian devils but, in some respects at least, businessmen seem much more likely to be patsies than predators.

For years now, the Capital Research Center in Washington has been documenting how corporate America has been bankrolling all sorts of left-leaning groups, whose programs attack or undermine the free market in general and corporations in particular. When developers subsidize environmental extremists, and employers contribute money to groups seeking to have government deny those employers the right to hire whatever individuals can do the job best, then something very strange is going on.

An even stranger, and perhaps more dangerous, development has been the hiring of so-called "diversity consultants" by big-name corporations all across the country.

These "diversity consultants" will come in to harangue your employees with the latest trendy notions on race and ethnicity. Or they will arrange weekend retreats where they can browbeat the staff and management. They put out brochures, videotapes, newsletters, or anything else that will send out The Word and bring in the money.

These professional intimidator don't come cheap. The more skilled or brazen of them charge thousands of dollars per day—and many will not work by the day, but insist on a long-term contract.

What are their skills? What are their credentials? What benefits can they promise?

Their skills are considerable. They have been known to reduce some employees to tears with their badgering, sneers and insinuations, just as they have been known to reduce some college students to tears when they take their act onto the campus.

They are great at laying on guilt trips or getting personal in a nasty way. Often they treat adults like children—or like guinea pigs.

Sometimes they ask the employees to line up and those who are religious to step to the right, those who believe that they are not racists to step forward, and so on. Above all, the "diversity" types do not discuss on the same plane with others. They lay down the social dogma from on high.

Credentials? Merely asking such a question is like asking to be accused of "insensitivity," if not racism. There are no formal credentials required to be known as a "diversity consultant." Effrontery and gall are pretty much the essentials. They are the secular versions of Elmer Gantry.

What benefits do they promise to employers? Usually nothing tangible that you can see any time soon. That would be "simplistic"—and not very profitable to the consultants.

The relationship between employees of different racial and ethnic backgrounds is supposed to be a great mystery, whose unraveling will require much time and much "re-education."

Black and white employees who were watching the same TV programs at home the previous night, and perhaps eating the same junk food at the mall during lunchtime, are taught to think of each other as exotic creatures from different worlds—unable to understand each other, except with the painful and expensive help of "diversity consultants."

How did businesses—or the country—manage to keep from coming apart all those years before these secular messiahs arrived on the scene? More important, why doesn't someone demand that they put up or shut up?

Have businesses—or colleges—that go in for this kind of bombast had happier relations among the various racial, ethnic or other groups afterwards? Or is it always "too early to see results yet"? In academia, the results seem to be that colleges which go in for this kind of brainwashing have more intergroup strife than before and more than colleges where no such programs exist.

Businesses that persist in subjecting their employees to this kind of indignity may see lawsuits for stress before they see any tangible benefits. As one who deplores the litigation explosion, I nevertheless think a few multimillion dollar damage awards would be a very healthy thing, to help restore sanity and common decency where these qualities are currently taking a back seat to being on the side of the politically correct angels.

Both the patterns of corporate philanthropy to their political enemies and the susceptibility of corporate management to such unproven nostrums as "diversity consultants" may suggest a death-wish to the more psychologically inclined. A more rationalistic explanation might be that it is all for the sake of public relations, even if the top corporate executives themselves think it is bunk.

Whatever the explanation, it is bad business in the long run, not only for business itself but for this country.

THE PRICE OF LIFE

THE TRAGIC EARTHQUAKE THAT HAS KILLED more than 25,000 people in India was not as large as the 1989 earthquake in California that killed fewer than a hundred people.

The difference is that Californians are affluent enough to build their homes, buildings, and other structures to earthquake-resistant standards, while the poverty-stricken people of India are not. Moreover, California has far more rescue equipment, more motor vehicles to rush people to hospitals, and far better medical facilities waiting in those hospitals.

Wealth is one of the greatest savers of lives, whether in earthquakes or in a thousand other ways. Put differently, stifling the production of wealth can cost more lives than many of the things that "safety" fanatics are creating hysteria about.

One of the grandiloquent phrases used to silence those who complain about the economic costs of government policies to reduce some remote danger is this: "It's worth it, no matter what it costs, if it saves just one human life!"

This kind of talk may allow the anointed to feel nobler than thou, but stifling the economy with safety regulations—killing the goose that lays the golden egg—will itself cost human lives. A faster growing economy can easily save more lives than trying to stamp out some danger that affects very few people, if it affects anybody.

Neither the public nor the media seem to be aware of how many professional hysteria-mongers there are with a vested interest in exaggerating every remote danger and inventing other dangers out of thin air. Unfortunately, the media's own vested interest in hype makes it all too willing to amplify whatever hysteria will sell newspapers or get more viewers to watch the tube.

Remember the Three Mile Island nuclear power plant "disaster" of 1987? Since then, scientific study after scientific study has failed to show how anybody suffered any concrete physical injury from that nuclear power plant accident, which is routinely referred to as a "disaster" in the media.

The only substantiated damage to people has been through stress and two deaths of people trying to flee the area. In short, more people were hurt by the media hysteria than by the accident itself.

Phantom Risk is the apt title of a new book published at M.I.T., detailing how all sorts of fictitious dangers have been hyped, not only in the media, but in courts of law as well. Only belatedly have the courts begun to restrict the half-baked theories and phoney "studies" that have been accepted as evidence in megabucks law suits.

Stuff that would never be accepted for publication in any reputable scientific, medical, or economic journal is accepted in courtrooms where multimillion dollar lawsuits are decided and whole industries crippled by the decisions.

It's called "junk science" in the law, but it's still considered money in the bank in the news business. Nothing would be easier than for the big television networks to hire their own group of statisticians and scientists to evaluate the stuff being turned out by innumerable organizations with much to gain by stampeding the public and the Congress into giving them money and power to deal with some artificial "crisis."

The Heritage Foundation in Washington has already shot down many of the manufactured alarums created by organizations that want laws and money to forward their own pet projects.

Merely keeping a record of the alarming predictions turned out regularly over the years by organizations like The Worldwatch Institute, or by individuals like Paul Ehrlich of Stanford, would be enough to produce a healthy skepticism, instead of the utter gullibility which has become the norm in the media.

Perhaps most of all, what is needed is an awareness that risks are inescapable in life and that trying to stamp out the last vestige of Risk A is opening yourself up to an increase in Risk B.

For example, you can get rid of all asbestos—and face increased risks of fire. You can ban all pesticides—and face a resurgence of malaria and other insect-borne diseases.

You can insist on long and costly years of testing of pharmaceutical drugs before they can be sold to the public—and watch many people die needlessly for lack of the drugs while you try to make something that is 99 percent safe become 99.5 percent safe. But of course nothing will ever be 100 percent safe, no matter how long you wait and how much you test.

If we can only start to think in terms of trade-offs instead of illusory "solutions," there may be some hope of sanity. Indeed, it would be quite an improvement if we could only start to think at all, instead of being swept along by rhetoric.

MEANINGLESS "EQUALITY"

IF ONE CONFUSED WORD CAN GUM UP SOCIAL POLICIES, the legal system, and innumerable institutions throughout society, that word is "equality." It is one of those vague pieties in which we indulge ourselves, without any serious thought as to what it means or what the actual consequences of pursuing it may be.

Anyone who questions or opposes equality is almost certain to be regarded as someone who believes in inequality—in "inferiority" and "superiority." But all three of these concepts suffer from the same problem: For equality, inferiority, or superiority to have any meaning, what is being compared must first be commensurable. A symphony is not equal to an automobile. Nor is it inferior or superior. They are simply not commensurable.

Much of the emotional struggle to make women "equal" to men suffers from the same problem. So long as women have babies and men do not, the many ramifications of that difference cannot be ignored and nothing can make them commensurable. However unisex one's language may be, women are seldom very good men and men cannot be women at all.

We may regard the happiness and well-being of women as equally important as the happiness and well-being of men—and probably most people do, despite shrill cries to the contrary—but that is a statement about our value system, not about some empirical reality of women and men.

With many other groups as well, the fundamental difference between equal treatment and equal performance is repeatedly confused. In performance terms, virtually no one is equal to anyone. The same individual is not even equal to himself on different days.

Much of the moral heartburnings, social engineering, and legal entanglements of our times comes from the simple fact that statistics for different groups are different in different occupations, institutions, or income levels. It is assumed automatically that only different treatment before the fact can explain different results after the fact.

This dogma is so deeply imbedded that it seems almost Utopian to attempt a rational discussion of it. Yet it was wholly arbitrary to have expected performance equality in the first place—and compounded pig-headedness to want to punish someone because it didn't happen. But there is a whole class of people who believe that when the world doesn't conform to their theory, that shows that something is wrong with the world.

Let us go back to the fact that women have babies, a fact of no small importance to those of us parochial enough to be concerned about the survival of the human species. Not only do women have babies, they realize in advance that they are likely to have babies— and those who are not yet "liberated" arrange their lives with that prospect in mind.

Occupations which require continuous employment to maintain ever-changing skills tend to attract fewer women than occupations they can leave to have children and return to later. You can take a few years off to see your children through the pre-school years and then return to become a good librarian, teacher, or editor, but take a few years off from computer engineering and you will return to find that you are not in Kansas anymore, Toto.

Some years ago, an economist investigated the rates of obsolescence of a wide range of occupations. A physicist lost half the value of his original knowledge in about five years, while it would take an historian more than 30 years to fall that far behind. Although the economist did not point this out—whether through oversight or prudence—the occupations with high rates of obsolescence were often "male dominated," while the occupations that are heavily female tended to have slow rates of obsolescence.

Although differences in choices and performances are ignored or dismissed in politically correct quarters, such differences obviously affect differences in outcomes, not only as between men and women but among racial, ethnic, and other groups as well.

Since it is truly Utopian to expect to have a rational discussion of inter-racial differences in these times, we can look at two branches of the same race—northern Europeans and southern Europeans.

For the past few centuries, northern Europeans have been far more advanced industrially and technologically than southern Europeans—not only in Europe itself, but when they immigrate to European-offshoot societies in the Western Hemisphere or Australia. But, for a thousand years or so before that, southern Europeans were far more advanced than northern Europeans.

In short, performances vary not only from individual to individual, but also from group to group, and from one era to another. Seldom are performances equal at any given moment.

In performance terms, Japan was decidedly inferior to the West in industrial technology a century ago. No one was more painfully aware of this than the Japanese themselves. That is what spurred them on to the efforts which have enabled them to overtake the West in many fields today.

They understood that this was not a problem that could be solved by lofty talk or arbitrary presuppositions.

MICRO-MANAGING MICROSOFT

RECENTLY I BOUGHT A COMPUTER that was identical to one that I purchased last year—except that it now costs $2,000 less. This has been a common pattern in the computer industry, where quality has gone up while prices have come down. At the other end of the spectrum, cars today cost what houses used to cost.

The automobile industry was once like the computer industry is today. That was back in the early part of the century, when Henry Ford was bringing the price of cars down to a level where ordinary people could afford them.

One of the big differences between these two industries is that politicians discovered the automobile as an issue back in the 1960s and have been trying to micro-manage it ever since. Features have to be added, not because the consumer wants them, but because people like Ralph Nader and the environmentalists can whip up political hysteria that translates into laws and bureaucratic regulation—and higher prices.

Safety was the entering wedge for the politicization of the auto-mobile—not real safety in the real world but promised safety in a "virtual reality" world. In that world, created by rhetoric and visions, the helpless and gullible consumer's safety has been sacrificed to "corporate greed" and only the knights in shining armor of the con-sumer movement can rescue him.

But during the pre-Nader era, automobile fatalities per passenger-mile declined by more than two-thirds while cars were driving faster and faster on more and more highways. Obviously, the decline since then has had to be less, despite much political fanfare about the "lives saved" by government-mandated safety requirements.

These calculations of "lives saved" depend on an implicit as-sumption that there was a static situation, to which "change" was added. In fact, the trend in fatality rates was downward for decades on end, so the continuation of that trend can hardly be credited to the spread of government mandates since the 1960s. In some years since federal regulation, fatality rates have moved up, but of course no one in Washington takes credit for that.

Until recently, politicians and bureaucrats have paid little or no attention to the computer industry. Now it has attracted the attention of phrase-makers ("information superhighway," "cyberspace," etc.), politicians, bureaucrats and judges. This has often been a fatal com-bination.

The Microsoft Corporation, whose operating systems run more than four fifths of the computers in the world, has been the focus of antitrust litigation, judicial murmurings and media malaise. What is remarkable is how few hard facts there are to substantiate all the theories, heartburnings and innuendoes.

The worry has been that Microsoft would be "unfair" to competitors or use its "market power" to "monopolize" the industry or do other equally vague and often undefinable things. At the heart of all this is a confusion between injuring competitors and injuring competition.

When competition is working as a process, some competitors are almost certain to be hurt. Those for whom equality is not just an ideal but a dogma simply cannot accept this. Sinister theories are one result of their attempts to reconcile their dogma with a reality that repeatedly mocks it.

The nebulous charges brought against Microsoft seem to boil down to the fact that Bill Gates runs the company's business for the benefit of the Microsoft Corporation, even when this is to the detriment of competitors. Shocking as this may seem to those in the cloistered world of academe or in the chambers of some federal judges, it is about what most people would expect in most other places.

For example, by including in the new Windows 95 software various programs which other companies sell separately, Microsoft may indeed displace some of those competitors from the market. But anyone who opens up a restaurant on the corner may take customers away from some other restaurant. Some people buy *Forbes* magazine instead of other business publications.

Promoting competition as a process is the opposite of promoting the survival of existing competitors. Unless and until public policy clearly and fully recognizes that fact, fanciful crusades and sinister theories will drive public policy towards the computer industry— and drive up the costs of that industry. If so, then the next time I buy the same model of computer, it may cost $2,000 more instead of $2,000 less.

FAMOUS PAIRS

SUCH FAMOUS PAIRS AS PUNCH AND JUDY, Gilbert and Sullivan and Abbott and Costello have their modern political counterparts in "the rich" and "the poor." No political campaign is complete without this famous pair and they make many cameo appearances in between elections, whenever almost any economic issue comes up.

While other pairs may have appeared to the accompaniment of music, "the rich" and "the poor" appear increasingly to the accompaniment of statistics. In the political arena, at least, their very existence is largely statistical. There are genuinely rich and genuinely poor people in the real world, but they bear little resemblance to their statistical counterparts in politics, where such terms typically refer to the top and bottom 10 or 20 percent of income earners.

Income distribution data are often a textbook example of the misuse of statistics. First of all, the very title is misleading, for most income is not distributed but earned. But that is only the beginning of the deception.

Economist Walter Williams has said that the way to tell if a politician is lying is to see if his lips are moving. One of the ways to tell if income statistics are deceptive is to see if they are presented as family and household income, rather than individual income or per capita income. Those who want to trumpet inequalities almost invariably choose family and household statistics.

For example, the real income of households in the United States was virtually the same in 1992 as in 1969, providing much fodder for those who proclaim economic stagnation, the disappearance of the middle class and miscellaneous other catastrophes. However, the real income per person in the United States grew by about 40 percent over that same span of time.

The reason for this paradox is that the average family size and average household size were declining. As individual incomes rose and more people could afford to move out and get their own places, those remaining behind had their incomes rising enough to offset the lost income of those who left. That is an increase in per capita income—not stagnation.

For groups such as blacks, whose family and household size have declined especially sharply, family and household statistics are particularly misleading.

Real income per black household rose only 7 percent between 1967 and 1988, and black household income was a lower percentage of white household income at the end of that period than at the beginning. But individual data show a radically different picture. Real income per black person increased by 81 percent over the same span of time and the average income of black individuals was a higher percentage of white individuals' average income at the end than at the beginning.

Needless to say, this leaves a lot of leeway for choosing your statistics to fit the political occasion, not only in Washington but also in the media and in academe.

But what about our heroes, "the rich" and "the poor"?

Those who think of people in the top and bottom 10 or 20 percent of income-earners this way have already fallen into a trap. Studies show, for example, that less than 20 percent of those in the bottom 20 percent actually stay there for as long as a decade. Many go all the way to the top 20 percent in that time. "The rich" are hardly less changeable and so are the people in the brackets in between, most of whom also do not stay put.

More than that, when we talk about the top 20 percent, we are not talking about the privileged but about those who work—shocking as that concept may be in an era when "work" is one of the few four-letter words that is considered to be in bad taste.

Just as families differ in size, they differ in working. Families in the top 20 percent supply 29 percent of all the people who work 50 weeks a year or more. Families in the bottom 20 percent supply just 7 percent of such people. How shocked should we be to discover that working brings in more money than not working? How much of an inequity is it?

The other striking thing about those who carry on about "the rich" and "the poor" is that they seldom say what kind of money they are actually talking about.

Even for total household income, you can make the top 20 percent with just over $58,000 and the top 5 percent with just under $100,000. A hundred grand is perhaps one successful professional, during his peak years, with his wife staying home with the kids. Or it may be two people working in modestly prosperous occupations. These are "the rich" that we hear so much about—from media pundits with six- and seven-figure incomes.

A study back in 1988 showed that a net worth of $112,000 was enough to put a household in the top 20 percent. Not a big market there for Rolls Royces.

Unlike politicians, media commentators and academicians don't even have to move their lips to lie. They can just present their selected statistics and let them "speak for themselves."

HOW "RICH" IS RICH?

WITH ALL THE TALK ABOUT "THE RICH" AND "THE POOR," you would think that someone would have defined these terms by now, so that we would all know what we are talking about. Not so.

What matters politically is what emotions these terms evoke and what policies, power and election prospects can be based on those emotions. Clarity would only undermine the political game.

A recent book about the rich—*The Millionaire Next Door*— sheds some very revealing light on this subject. First of all, it defines what it means by rich, which is more than Congressional demagogues do when they thunder against "tax cuts for the rich," who include millions of mechanics, construction workers, government employees and other middle-class people.

Authors Thomas Stanley and William Danko define the rich as people whose net worth is one million dollars or more. Some of us could quibble about that figure, since net worth counts everything, including the kitchen sink. It also includes the money in your pension fund, the value of your car, the equity in your home and other wealth that you are not likely to be able to turn into ready cash.

Nevertheless, the fact that a million dollars is a definite number is such an improvement over other sloppy uses of the term "rich" that we can at least talk sense about the subject. First of all, we can ask: How many rich are there and how did they get that way?

Even by the modest definition in *The Millionaire Next Door*, only about 3.5 percent of American households are rich and 80 percent of these millionaires earned the money themselves. The classic millionaire of Hollywood movie fame—born in a mansion, heir to a fortune, educated at snooty private schools and Ivy League colleges—is the exception, rather than the rule.

The authors confess that they themselves started out with these stereotypes about the rich and were repeatedly shocked by what they actually found. Even a meeting that a big financial organization had them arrange for people who each had $10 million or more in assets—now we are really talking rich—turned out to be a fiasco because most of the people who came were not used to the posh setting and fancy food and drink that had been prepared for them.

Many of the rich do not live in "gold coast" neighborhoods but among ordinary middle-class and working class people. That is the reason for the title of the book, *The Millionaire Next Door*. Nor do most of these millionaires drive big luxury cars. The average cost of their cars is $24,800—about $4,000 more than the average cost of other Americans' cars, but far below the cost of a Cadillac or Lexus, much less a Rolls Royce.

The "lifestyle of the rich and famous" does exist, but not all of those who live it are either rich or famous. One of the millionaires used an old Texas expression for showy people without much behind their show—"Big hat, no cattle."

Nor are all the professional athletes or entertainers with megabucks salaries going to end up rich in their old age. There have already been too many sad stories of famous boxers, movie stars and others who made millions and either spent it all or were gypped out of it.

Most millionaires did not get their money from megabucks salaries, inheritance or winning a lottery or quiz show prize. Most have been self-employed, worked like dogs to build up their earnings and then saved most of it.

Half the millionaires surveyed never paid as much as $400 for the most expensive suit they ever bought. The ones who earned the money paid less and the ones who inherited it paid more. For every millionaire who buys a $1,000 suit, 6 or more non-millionaires buy one.

Unlike too many other studies of income and wealth in America, *The Millionaire Next Door* is a study of flesh-and-blood people, not statistics in which the top 20 percent are arbitrarily called "the rich" and the bottom 20 percent "the poor." Most of the people in both these brackets do not spend their lives in such brackets.

Only about 3 percent of the American population remains in the bottom 20 percent for as long as 8 years. Add that to the 3.5 percent who are rich, and you end up with less than 7 percent of the American population being either rich or poor—even though great political battles are fought in the name of these small fractions of atypical people, instead of the other 93 percent of us.

BLOOD GUZZLERS

FOR YEARS NOW, THE MORALLY ANOINTED have been denouncing large automobiles as "gas guzzlers," and the Clinton administration is committed to legislating higher gas mileage requirements. The most likely consequence of all this is that our cars will go from being gas guzzlers to being blood guzzlers.

There is no mystery about how to get higher gas mileage: Build smaller and lighter cars. And there is no mystery as to what happens when people have automobile accidents in lighter cars: They are more likely to be killed or severely injured.

Mileage mania means trading blood for oil.

The insurance industry keeps careful tabs on who gets injured driving what kinds of cars, because they have millions of dollars at stake. According to data from the Insurance Institute for Highway Safety, if you drive one of those big old gas guzzlers like a Cadillac or a Lincoln Town Car, your chances of filing an insurance claim for severe injury is about half of what it is for a driver of a Ford Escort or Hyundai Excel.

It's not a question of a particular manufacturer or a particular brand. Large luxury cars in general—gas guzzlers—average less than half the severe injury claims of small two-door automobiles.

With all the money you save on gas by driving smaller and lighter cars, you may be able to afford a longer stay in the hospital or a fancier funeral.

None of this should be a surprise to anyone. Life is one trade-off after another. There are no "solutions," even though intellectuals and politicians are constantly talking as if there were.

How desperate are we to save gasoline—and why?

The world's known petroleum reserves today are double what they were in 1969. This may sound strange to those who have been

69

listening to the political hysteria of the past 20 years, but political panic-mongers are rarely concerned about the facts.

With petroleum, as with many other natural resources, someone is always saying that our current supply will run out in 10 years or 20 years, or whatever other number they can concoct. At best, these numbers reflect nothing more than sheer ignorance of economics.

At worst, they represent a calculated attempt to start a political stampede toward whatever policy is being promoted, for whatever ulterior purpose.

Natural resources do not jump up out of the ground and announce where they are located. Looking costs money. Drilling a lot of dry holes before you finally strike oil costs money.

Seldom will it make sense economically to invest so many millions of dollars in looking for petroleum (or other natural resources) as to locate enough to last for centuries. Depending on the interest rate charged on investment funds, as well as other factors, it may only pay to locate enough of the resource to last 15 or 20 years.

That is why panic-mongers are able to go around crying that we will be "running out" of some vital natural resource in 15 or 20 years.

As the inventory of a natural resource declines, then it pays to go look for some more, so that the point at which we are theoretically going to "run out" always recedes before us, like the horizon. We certainly did not have a fifty-year supply of known petroleum reserves fifty years ago—nor was there any reason why we should have.

The problem is not simply that rhetoric is more popular than economics. The more fundamental problem is that there are whole classes of people whose whole role in life, and whose egos, depend on their seeming to be so much wiser, nobler, more "concerned," and more "compassionate" than the rest of us.

They are forever looking for ways for the government to impose their superior wisdom and virtue on the benighted masses. For years, they have been carrying on a veritable war against the automobile, which represents the very antithesis of their vision of how the world should be run.

Instead of having the anointed looking down from on high, and directing the ant-like creatures below as to how they should travel to and fro, we have a world where ordinary Americans can decide when, where, and how to go, without so much as a "by your leave" to their betters in Washington, in the academy, or in the media.

The automobile has been one of the great liberating forces of the twentieth century. It did more to reduce severe overcrowding, common in cities a century ago, than all the hand-wringing reformers put together. But, as the automobile enabled people to spread out into the suburbs, to get some elbow room, the anointed began to wring their hands over what they now chose to call "urban sprawl."

People living cramped lives, whether in cities or in rural areas, had whole new vistas opened up to them by the automobile. Many could now travel around the country, some visiting the vacation resorts or national parks once reserved for the elite.

The elite in fact began to complain about places that were now "spoiled" because the great unwashed intruded into their exclusive little worlds. Environmentalism owes much to this elite resentment, and the rhetoric of trying to "save" this or "preserve" that is often nothing more than selfishness posing as nobility.

Automobiles are no more exempt from trade-offs than anything else in this world. This has allowed the anointed to seize upon every cost that goes with the benefits of the automobile, whether pollution, safety problems, or the "using up" of petroleum.

Everything that uses fuel produces pollution, including the horses that automobiles replaced. Horse manure was a far more serious pollution problem in American cities than the exhaust fumes of today.

Indeed, the horse manure of today's anointed is still polluting the political process—and may well succeed in turning gas guzzlers into blood guzzlers.

BRINGING DOWN THE DEFICIT

"HI, BOB. WELL, HERE WE GO AGAIN."

"Got all your W-2's and other tax records, Tom?"

"Well, I think they are all here."

"You think? In other words, you don't know."

"I suppose you could put it that way. You accountants are a tough bunch."

"All right. I guess uncertainty is what makes doing Tom Sowell's income taxes such an adventure."

"Don't worry, Bob. I'm getting my financial affairs together."

"Really?"

"Yeah, I was inspired by the President's speech the other night."

"How so?"

"I plan to get solvent by reducing my spending and increasing my revenues, just like the government."

"How are you going to do that?"

"First of all, I plan to cut my staff by five people."

"Wait a minute, Tom. You only have two people working for you. How can you cut your staff by five?"

"Well, you see I was planning to increase the staff to nine over the next few years, but now I'm going to increase it just to four. So that means I have cut my staff by five."

"Where did you get that crazy way of looking at things?"

"That's the way they figure it in Washington. A lot of the spending cuts in the President's budget are cuts in projections, not actual reductions in spending."

"You mean the spending goes up, but because it didn't go up as much as they originally projected, it's called a spending 'cut'?"

"Exactly."

"I knew your mind would crack if you kept on following politics."

"I am also going to save by cutting back on driving."

"Like, for instance?"

"Well, I had been planning to drive from California to Maine, but now I am only going to drive to Las Vegas. That's a cutback of about 2,000 miles."

"When was the last time you actually drove all the way across the country, Tom?"

"1969."

"When was the last time you even drove out of the state?"

"1975."

"So this is not an actual cutback in your driving. This is just a cutback in your driving plans."

"But I tell you, Bob, this is how they do it in Washington. What's good enough for the President of the United States is good enough for me."

"How do you plan to increase your revenues? Get rich by winning in Las Vegas?"

"Bob, a lot more people are rich than you think."

"I've been doing your income taxes for years, Tom. Believe me, you're not rich."

"Don't be so sure, Bob. The President said he was going to tax the rich, right?"

"Yes."

"And my taxes are going up, right?"

"You'd better believe it, Tom."

"Well, there you are."

"No, no. The 'rich' used to mean people making over $200,000 a year, but that came down to $100,000 last week—and all of that doesn't have to be cash income. For retired people, income taxes are going up for people making less than $30,000 a year."

"You accountants know everything. But you're only proving my point. Lots of people are rich now."

"Tom, anybody who's making $30,000 a year and thinks he is rich has big problems—and not just taxes."

"All right, so I'm not rich. But I can increase my revenue, just like the government is going to do."

"The government prints its own money. How are you going to do it?"

"I'm going to double what I charge for writing or giving speeches. That will give me twice as much additional revenue."

"What if some people won't pay it?"

"Bob, you're not with it. That's not how they figure things in Washington."

"How do they figure it?"

"They figure if they double the tax rate, they will have twice as much revenue."

"That's crazy. If they double the tax rate, people will come in here asking me how to put their money in tax shelters. The government will never collect twice as much revenue that way."

"But, Bob, that's how the government is planning to bring down the deficit. Are you against 'change'?"

"I like change. But I like paper money better."

UNFUNDED MANDATES

NOTHING SO EPITOMIZES CONTEMPORARY LIBERALISM as unfunded mandates, in which the federal government establishes programs and forces the states to pay for them. The very need to weigh benefits against costs—the essence of economics—is evaded by this irresponsible exercise of arrogance. It is like impulse buying and charging it to somebody else's credit card.

The great hysteria in the media about the wonderful programs that will be lost if unfunded mandates are stopped misses the whole point. If these programs are as wonderful as they are said to be, then they should be paid for. Nothing is easier than to make a verbal case for almost anything, but are you willing to put your money where your mouth is?

If you are not even willing to put the taxpayers' money where your mouth is, there is something wrong somewhere.

The number of things that are beneficial vastly exceeds what any nation can afford. That is why both individuals and organizations must weigh trade-offs all the time. Unfunded mandates, hidden taxes, and a whole range of environmental restrictions, are all ways of making costly decisions without having to weigh those costs against the benefits.

It is government by magic words, whether those words are "safety" "minimum wages," or "clean air."

Can anybody be against "safety"? Not verbally and not politically. But, in real life, do we go around in suits of armor?

Do we refuse to drive or ride in cars? Of course not. We weigh the risks against the benefits.

Only in grandiloquent political rhetoric do we claim that safety must be achieved at all costs. We can do it there only because those costs are to be paid by somebody else. When even the big spenders in Washington are not willing to pay from the federal treasury, then we have lost all sense of trade-offs. We have become like small children who want everything—and cry if we don't get it.

What is the minimum wage law but an unfunded mandate imposed on private organizations? If everyone deserves "a living wage" or "a decent standard of living," then why don't those who think that way supply these things? If it is "society's" responsibility to see that no one falls below some economic level, then why don't we raise the taxes and pay for that level?

Why is someone who runs a print shop or a bakery more responsible for other people's economic level than someone who works in a thousand other occupations? TV pundits and editorial office saints often make more money than the great majority of businessmen. Why single out employers to dump this responsibility on?

We all want clean air and water, don't we? The only problem is that there has never been any such thing. No water and no air has ever been 100 percent pure, at least not since Adam and Eve made the wrong decision back in the garden. There are different levels of impurities with different levels of consequences.

No one wants to breathe air full of sulphur or drink water with sewage in it, so it makes sense to remove some impurities—but not every trace of everything that every hysterical crusader can think of. There are wells being shut down by the government because they have traces of chemicals more minute than you can find in a bottle of soda or a can of beer.

Any one of us could make the air in his own home cleaner by installing all sorts of costly filters and we could eliminate many impurities in water by drinking only water that we distilled ourselves. But we don't do that, do we? We think it is too costly, whether in money or in time.

Only when we are putting costs on other people do we go hog wild like that. Making us pay is one way to make us think.

Environmental agencies have been having a field day putting restrictions on how other people can use their own property. These restrictions may cut the value of the property in half or even reduce it to zero. There is never a lack of pretty words to justify this.

But what if those agencies had to compensate the owner for the losses they have imposed on him?

If the restrictions' benefits to "society" outweigh the losses to the owner, then it makes sense to pay the money and everybody ends up better off. But when you confiscate property by the back door, you can just say some lofty words and keep going. You don't have to weigh anything against anything.

In reality, many of the things being financed by unfunded mandates or imposed on businesses and property owners are not for the benefit of "society." They are for the benefit of the careers or the egos of those who promote programs. That is why things that cannot be justified have to be financed under the table.

NO MONEY

IT SEEMS TO COME AS A BIG SHOCK to some people that money buys desirable things. But why else would people work for it? What other justification would there be for the government to use up so much green ink printing it?

In some of the loftier quarters, such as the editorial pages of the *New York Times,* it is considered terrible that people with less money cannot have all the things that people with more money have. The latest version of this complaint is that there will not be "full participation" in "the information society" if computer services over phone lines are not widely available because of the cost.

Among the supposedly heart-rending stories cited by the *N.Y. Times* is that a library serving four counties in the Adirondacks paid out $50,000 last year for data transmission services out of what was described as a "meager" budget. Putting aside the question as to how many of the poor and the downtrodden are living in the Adirondacks, if it cost 50 grand to give these counties what they wanted, why shouldn't they have to pay 50 grand to get it?

Why should somebody else somewhere else be paying for it?

Surely the editorial page pundits have not been breathing so many noxious fumes from Times Square traffic that they don't realize that somebody is going to have to pay for everything, one way or another. Why not have things paid for by the people who use them? One of the most obvious ways to let someone decide how much he really wants something is to make him put his money where his mouth is.

That $50,000 payment that the Times Square anointed find so heart-rending is, after all, just $12,500 per county. That's less than the cost of hiring one civil servant, yet no one finds it heart-rending for a county to have to pay its bureaucrats.

If firing just one part-time employee could cover a county's whole computer bill for a year, then let the county decide what it wants most. That is the whole point of money and of having to pay for what you use.

Trade-offs are not just something thought up by conservative meanies. As long as what we want exceeds what we have—and it's been that way for thousands of years now—we are going to have to make trade-offs. It doesn't matter whether you are a carpenter or a CEO, whether you are down in a submarine or up at the dizzying heights of an editorial office in Times Square.

Even those who bemoan the fact that money (or lack thereof) determines "access" to various desirable things cannot come right out and deny the need for trade-offs. They just want to exempt whatever they like from those trade-offs.

It is not just computer services that they want determined by the words of the anointed instead of the competition of the marketplace. They want all sorts of things in the environment "saved"—which is to say, prevented from being used by other people who, for some reason, are not supposed to have the same rights as the anointed.

Anything the environmental anointed want "saved" by political fiat could instead be saved by being purchased in competition with others who want to use it differently. But that would require the environmentalists to put their money where their mouth is. More fundamentally, it would put the environmentalists on the same plane as everyone else, instead of on the lofty heights they reserve for themselves.

Put differently, some people want to decide with words what the trade-offs will be for other people, instead of letting those others decide for themselves with money what they want and how much. In other words, power to the talkers!

Unfortunately, talk is one of the most treacherous ways of making decisions. Anybody can say anything but everybody cannot do everything. Few things are more dangerous than letting some people make decisions for which other people pay the costs.

Power-grabbers often hide behind the poor. The *New York Times* and the Clinton administration speak of "the information have nots," such as "the poorest of the poor" who lack telephones. Since basic telephone service costs less than booze or drugs, there is a serious question whether we are talking about a lack of "access" or about a different set of priorities.

The fact that people have alternatives and make choices is a very inconvenient fact for those with the vision of the anointed. They must constantly depict other people as helpless in order to justify their own grab for power.

The real problem with money is that it is the mechanism by which people make decisions that the anointed want to make for them.

AGE WARFARE

MY FAVORITE SALAD-BAR RESTAURANT HAS TWO LINES. Although I always get the same thing for lunch, I was puzzled at first to discover that I was charged $7.83 in one line and $8.49 in the other. The reason turned out to be that people over 55 years of age are given a discount—and apparently different cashiers judged my age differently.

When I entered Yosemite National Park recently, and was about to purchase my usual annual pass, I noticed that there was also a "golden age" pass for which I qualified. The annual pass to Yosemite costs $25 but the "golden age" pass was only $10—and it is good for the rest of my life in all national parks.

Such age discrimination is the fruit of relentless propaganda campaigns of the 1980s about "the poor and the elderly." What makes it a farce is that the elderly hold most of the nation's wealth.

Households headed by someone from 55 to 64 years old average more than twice the net worth of households headed by someone aged 35 to 44—which in turn average more than twice the net worth of households headed by someone under 35. Studies over the past 30 years have shown repeatedly that the only age bracket which consistently has more than 20 percent of its members earning more than double the national average income is the age bracket from 45 to 54 years old.

Despite the reality, image carries more weight in politics, and the image of the elderly poor makes the many privileges of older people sacrosanct. It is not just the political muscle of the American Association of Retired Persons, it is the neutralization of younger voters with pathetic images of the elderly that enable such Robin-Hood-in-reverse policies to persist and expand.

Nothing is more sacrosanct than Social Security—or more grossly a transfer of wealth from those with less to those with more. It is in fact one of the political miracles of the 20th century. Sold to the public as an "insurance" plan in which people get back what they paid in, it has instead operated like a pyramid club, with those who came in early getting money from those who came in later.

Like most pyramid schemes, Social Security worked like a charm at first. The growing number of young workers paying Social Security taxes enabled retirees to draw pensions out of all proportion to what they themselves had put it in, and enabled Congress to think up new goodies with which to sweeten the Social Security package.

Now, as the retirement of the huge baby-boomer generation looms ahead on the horizon, so do huge financial problems for the Social Security system. None of this would have happened if Social Security had been what it pretended to be—an insurance plan. If people were just getting back what they paid in, there would be no financial problem, whether or not more people joined later.

Obviously, you cannot just pull the rug out from under retired people who relied on Social Security to help see them through the years when they no longer have a paycheck. But, equally, there is no reason to set fraudulent promises in concrete for all eternity.

In order to take Social Security out of the realm of the sacrosanct, it will be necessary to guarantee existing retired people that they will not lose a dime—and to extend the same guarantee to those in the decade leading up to retirement. The time is also long overdue to stop pretending that this is some kind of insurance when it is in fact just another government transfer program, with no more moral basis than farm subsidies or welfare.

Once we face up to the plain fact that Social Security is welfare for the elderly, then we need to ask ourselves why affluent people of any age should be a burden on others. They should not be.

For those whose retirement has been planned with Social Security checks in mind, pay them whatever they are currently receiving. But pay it out of general tax revenues, not out of special Social Security "contributions" which are nothing more than a regressive tax on young working people. Those who are at or near retirement age should also not be left out on the limb but bailed out with general tax revenues.

This should obviously be a one-time operation to ease the transition to a more honest and rational approach to old age. In other words, we should stop promising pie in the sky to younger people who will never get back what they paid in.

It is also time to start charging people who use the national parks what it costs to maintain those parks for their use, regardless of whether they are in their twenties or in their sixties.

MISUNDERSTANDING THE MARSHALL PLAN

THE 50TH ANNIVERSARY OF THE MARSHALL PLAN was guaranteed to bring out of the woodwork all the shallow and noisy people who think that government programs are the answer to all problems. These people include one of the shallowest and noisiest of them all, Julianne Malveaux of *U.S.A. Today* and assorted talk shows.

According to Ms. Malveaux, we should "try to transform nations the way we did with the Marshall Plan." We can also "replicate the Marshall Plan at home" in our inner cities. This mindset shows a complete ignorance or disregard of history.

A hundred years before the Marshall Plan, John Stuart Mill pointed out that nations often have apparently miraculous recoveries from the devastations of war because the physical destruction did not include destruction of the skills, experience and aptitudes which built the physical things in the first place.

In short, what is crucial is the "human capital" needed to build or rebuild the physical things. What the Marshall Plan did was to help feed and house people in Western Europe until they could rebuild— using the "human capital" that they already had and which had built Western Europe into one of the leading industrial regions of the world in the first place.

Where that "human capital" does not exist, you can pour untold billions down a bottomless pit without making a dent in the problem. Nothing has been more common in Third World countries than rusting machinery from the industrial world, whether left over from the days of colonialism or built with foreign aid from the West. As John Stuart Mill saw in the 19th century, it is not the physical capital but the human capital that is crucial.

The same thing was true even further back in history, when the Romans pulled out of Britain in the 5th century, leaving intact a physical infrastructure which they had built—but which the British, at that juncture in history, did not have the human capital to maintain. Buildings and roads fell into disrepair and, in some places, forests and wildness began to grow back into what had been human settlements under the Romans.

None of this is hard to understand from an intellectual point of view. What is hard is to give up the emotionally satisfying vision of moral melodrama that holds such fascination for sophomores of all ages, including Ms. Malveaux.

According to this moral melodrama, the poor are poor because of what the rich have taken from them. Hence all the heady talk about "liberation" and various esoteric theories of "exploitation."

According to Malveaux, Africa's downfall "was European colonialism." If this were to be taken as a serious statement to be tested against the facts, it would immediately collapse like a house of cards. So would most other exploitation theories.

If Europeans made Africa poor, then the departure of these Europeans, as African nations emerged into independence in the 1960s, should have led to rising standards of living. Tragically, in most of sub-Saharan Africa, standards of living were lower 20 years after the imperialists were gone.

In Central Asia likewise, freedom from Russian domination after the break-up of the Soviet Union did not bring rising standards of living but falling standards of living. Most of the scientific, technological, and managerial skills in Central Asia did not belong to Central Asians but primarily to Russians.

Similar results are seen, again and again, when various minority groups who are supposed to be "exploiting" others are expelled from countries around the world. In medieval Europe, Jews were expelled from a number of countries where they were accused of exploiting the gentiles. But, after they left, prices and interest rates tended to rise.

Exploitation does take place and oppression still more so. But they seldom explain either the wealth of the wealthy or the poverty of the poor.

Spain, for example, exploited the Western Hemisphere and its people mercilessly for centuries. But after the gold and silver ran out and the Indians died off, Spain had very little to show for it and has remained one of the poorer countries in Europe. It not only failed to develop its own human capital, it expelled minorities whose human capital had contributed to the Spanish economy, including both the Jews and the Moors.

Although human capital fits the facts better than moral melodrama, it presents no sweeping solutions for politicians to offer and no heady feeling of superiority for the intelligentsia. So look for more calls for more Marshall Plans.

PART III
THE POLITICAL SCENE

GOVERNMENT VERSUS PROGRESS

ONE OF THE CURIOUS FACTS about the history of technology is how many fundamental inventions began in China but were developed further in Europe. The compass, gunpowder and printing all appeared in China centuries before they appeared in Europe, and the Chinese were producing vast amounts of iron long before the Europeans. Yet Europe not only caught up with China, in these and other fields, but vastly outstripped it.

Among the many areas in which China was far in advance of Europe for many centuries was government. After Western Europe fragmented politically with the collapse of the Roman Empire, no government there ruled nearly so vast an area as the government in China. Nor did European rulers have as effective control over the territory that they did rule.

In both Europe and China, governments wanted to regulate and control the marketplace—notions of a "just price" appeared in both places—and to siphon off the wealth that would otherwise accumulate in private hands. It was just that in China the government was capable of carrying out its intentions and in much of Western Europe it was not.

The political fragmentation of Europe meant that rulers had to compete for wealth-producing subjects, so as to acquire through taxation the means to promote their own military power.

While arbitrary confiscations and other acts of spoliation occurred in both parts of the world, and both were capable of suffocating levels of interference in the marketplace, the Chinese were not nearly as restrained by the need to compete for wealth-producing subjects.

In medieval Europe, this competition was not restricted to competition for truly rich merchants and bankers. Rulers in Eastern Europe, for example, made conscious efforts to attract peasants and artisans from Western Europe, and especially from Germany. In many cases, these peasants and artisans were allowed to live in numerous ethnic enclaves, both urban and rural, under the laws they were accustomed to in Western Europe, rather than the more restrictive laws to which the peoples of Eastern Europe were subjected.

So widespread were these Western European enclaves in Eastern Europe that most of the medieval cities of that region had majority populations that were ethnically different from the majority population of the surrounding countryside. Cracow's official records, for example, were kept in German until 1312 (when they began to be kept in Latin) and it was generations later before Poles became a majority in the city.

Western Europeans were in demand in Eastern Europe partly because they were more advanced technologically and therefore produced more wealth per capita, to the ultimate benefit of the governments and rulers of the region. Partly they were in demand simply because of vastly greater amounts of virgin land that would otherwise lie idle in Eastern Europe.

Within Western Europe the competition for wealth-producing subjects was fierce. Ports that imposed high tariffs saw ships go to other ports. Rulers who confiscated found themselves with less and less to confiscate. Cities and states where laws were unreliable or biased against foreigners saw wealth and commerce go to places like London, where the reputation of British law for fairness and impartiality attracted bankers and merchants from other parts of Europe.

The large amounts of capital needed to finance technological development could be safely accumulated in private hands in at least parts of Europe, whereas such private fortunes had much less chance of survival under the heavy-handed Chinese government and a society with Confucian disdain toward commerce. The nobility and the intelligentsia of Europe were equally disdainful of commerce, but competition among governments limited how far that disdain could translate into law and policy.

Personal freedom also emerged as concessions made in the competition for people. For European rulers, this was a matter of expediency, but for the people themselves this became a matter of principle and right.

In short, European rulers were forced by circumstances to create both greater personal freedom and greater freedom of the marketplace than existed in China or in most other parts of the world. The enormous power of those two factors was shown by Europe's overtaking of China in field after field where the Chinese first excelled.

FREEDOM VERSUS DEMOCRACY

THE ONLY TIME I HAVE LEFT a court room with more respect for the law than I had going in was in a court in Hong Kong, when it was under British colonial rule.

The case involved a Chinese laborer accused of theft, an accusation with considerable circumstantial evidence behind it. This case was presided over by a crusty old British judge, of upper-class demeanor and wearing the traditional white wig. He kept both lawyers on a short leash and let the witnesses know too that he had no tolerance for nonsense.

It would be hard to find two individuals more different in background and status than the Chinese laborer on trial and the British judge in charge of the case. Yet race and class were not destiny, despite the current dogmas of our intelligentsia. What was clear from the outset was that the judge was determined to see that this man got a fair trial—no more and no less. In the end, the laborer was acquitted.

One need only look around the world today, much less back through the pages of history, to see how rare and precious something as basic as a fair trial has been. Whether or how long such trials will exist in Hong Kong under the Communists is another question, and a very painful one.

Meanwhile, too many Western journalists continue to play the game of moral equivalence: There was no democracy in Hong Kong under the British, they say, and there is no democracy there now. Some hark back to the evils of 19th century imperialism that led to Britain's acquiring Hong Kong in the first place. There seems to be much less interest in 20th century totalitarianism in China that sent so many refugees fleeing to Hong Kong, among other places.

Democracy and freedom are too often confounded. Britain itself did not have anything close to democracy until the Reform Act of 1832. But it had freedom long before that.

The fundamentals of freedom—limited government, separation of powers, an independent judiciary, free speech, jury trials—existed in Britain for many generations before the franchise was extended to most males. The whole spirit, and many of the phrases, of the Constitution of the United States derive from British law and government.

Just as freedom can exist without democracy, so democracy can crush freedom. During the Reconstruction era after the Civil War, blacks in the South had many rights that they lost when the occupying Union army was withdrawn and democratically-elected state governments took over, ushering in the Jim Crow era.

Today, the confusion between freedom and democracy leads far too many Americans, including those in high places, to seek to spread democracy around the world—in complete disregard of the circumstances of the particular countries. In some respects, we may be more dangerous to our friends than to our enemies, when we pressure them to set up at least the trappings of democracy.

Both freedom and democracy have prerequisites. When those prerequisites do not exist, democracy especially can be a house of cards.

Whether in Eastern Europe and the Balkans between the two World Wars or in Africa in the postwar era, many newly created democratic governments collapsed into authoritarianism or worse. It is much easier to imitate the outward institutional forms of Western democracy than to synthesize the centuries of traditions that make those institutions work.

Our insistence on at least a charade of democracy is dangerous in another way—to ourselves. Relations among nations, especially among the great powers, are not matters of personal friendship or international social work. Their primary goal is, or should be, the safety of the American people in a world that has always been dangerous, long before the Cold War came and went.

We cannot go around the world acting like a common scold, however good that makes us feel or however well it plays politically at home. Nuclear proliferation is far more important than "human rights" pronouncements—and how much cooperation we get in trying to deal with dangerous threats like this may depend on how much political capital we have squandered by insulting other countries whose help we need.

The British were very wise to have given Hong Kong freedom. But they may also have been wise in not attempting to experiment with democracy, where the traditions needed for it simply did not exist.

WILL CHEMICAL WEAPONS BE BANNED?

THE PROPOSED TREATY TO BAN CHEMICAL WEAPONS is another painful reminder of how easily we are misled by words. Who could possibly be against banning chemical weapons? The real question is whether this treaty—or any treaty—can actually do that.

Many people with military backgrounds, including past Secretaries of Defense Caspar Weinberger and James Schlesinger, oppose

Senate ratification of the treaty precisely because it will increase the dangers, rather than reduce them. Politicians from both parties have lined up on the opposite side, in favor of the treaty, because it makes more sense politically than it does militarily.

Politically, what is at stake is "American leadership" in the "new world order." In other words, our political leaders will have egg on their faces internationally if they cannot get this treaty ratified by the Senate—and that in turn will make it harder for them to exert influence in the future.

But, when it comes to what the treaty is supposedly about— banning chemical weapons—it is not merely inadvisable but downright dangerous.

Ask yourself: Why did Hitler not use chemical weapons against the Allies during World War II, especially since he had no qualms about chemically killing millions of defenseless civilians in his concentration camps? The answer is that he knew that gassing Americans would lead to Americans gassing far more Germans.

We had chemical weapons and he knew it. That is why Hitler didn't use his. There is nothing complicated about this—either then or now. What gets complicated is trying to evade the obvious, in the interest of scoring political points by being on the side of the angels and denouncing chemical weapons.

All weapons are harmful. That is what makes them weapons. It is short-sighted grandstanding for politicians to pretend to be banning weapons that they cannot in fact ban. But that is what makes them politicians.

The joker in all sorts of disarmament treaties throughout this century has been that peaceful nations tend to abide by them while aggressors violate them. That is how Britain got suckered in its naval treaty with Nazi Germany in the 1930s and how both Britain and the United States got suckered in their naval treaty with Japan before that.

Men paid with their lives during World War II for these pre-war political charades that allowed aggressor nations to gain military advantages while peaceful nations held back from building the military deterrents that were needed. For the first two years of that war, the democracies did not win a single major battle against the totalitarian powers—and not many minor battles either.

Eventually, the tide turned, after the United States belatedly began to build up its military forces, but it was touch and go for quite a while. In an age of devastating chemical and nuclear warfare, there may not be any second chances.

Some of the most dangerous countries in the world today are not even going to sign the so-called chemical weapons ban treaty. This is an invitation for us to disarm ourselves of a chemical weapons deterrent, while people like Saddam Hussein remain free to use theirs.

As for other major powers that plan to sign the treaty, how are we to verify whether they will live up to it? And even if we discover that China, for example, is not living up to the treaty, what can we do about it then? Start a war?

Even small powers can build up devastating chemical arsenals because they require no huge facilities. That is also why violations of the treaty can be very difficult to detect, until it is too late.

Why is something so militarily dangerous so politically popular? Mushy wishful thinking on the part of too many Americans, and a cynical exploitation of their feelings by politicians.

Every ban on any kind of weapon—nuclear, chemical or other— is sure to be greeted by cheers in the media. The specifics of these treaties receive little attention. Apparently it's the thought that counts.

Actually, it is the feelings that count politically, since very little thought goes into many of these feelings. Both at home and abroad, those who want weapons banned on paper seldom pause to think that peaceful people are much easier to disarm than violent people—and disarming peaceful people just shifts the balance of power in favor of aggressors, increasing the very dangers you are trying to reduce.

SUPPLY-SIDE POLITICS

DURING THE LONG YEARS when Keynesian economics reigned supreme, economists tended to try to explain the ups and downs of the economy almost entirely by what was happening to demand. Supply appeared to be just a passive response to whatever demand did. That of course set the stage for "supply-side economics," which emphasized the incentives to those who supplied output and jobs.

If Keynesian economics stressed the supposed benefits of having government manipulate aggregate demand, supply-side economics stressed what the marketplace could accomplish, once it was freed from government controls and taxes.

In too many other areas of our national life, we are still emphasizing the demand side, almost to the complete exclusion of the supply side. For example, political explanations of the kinds of policies followed by government typically focus on what the voters or the organized special interests want—the demand side. Little or no attention is paid to the supply side—that is, to the kinds of people who choose politics as a career and the kinds of policies such people are likely to prefer.

A few years ago, Alan Ehrenhalt's *The United States of Ambition* pointed out that conservative districts are often represented by liberal Congressmen, simply because the supply of people who want a career in government is weighted toward people who think it is important for government to play a large role in our lives.

In other words, you cannot explain the kinds of policies that come out of Washington simply by the electoral or financial pressures on politicians inside the Beltway. Some of them are due to the kinds of people who seek careers within the Beltway. The same reasoning would apply to Congressional staffers or to the kinds of people attracted toward a career in the federal judiciary.

Those highly skeptical of the role of government in general or the judiciary in particular are unlikely to have the same fire in the belly or to be as willing to sacrifice their families' financial well-being and privacy in pursuit of the levers of power. Even the notable exception of the militant conservative freshmen Congressmen elected in 1994 seems in some ways to prove the rule. These militant freshmen have pushed for term limits and some have not even bothered to buy homes in the Washington area. Initially, at least, they do not seem to be coming to Washington to settle in, like their liberal counterparts.

Much the same failure to consider the supply side badly affects our understanding of the problems of the American public school system. Here too, many observers try to explain the many failed policies and fads of the system by the theories of education gurus or by the demands of society.

Yet it is hard to see how any fundamental improvement in our public schools is likely, so long as those schools are supplied with teachers and administrators like the ones being turned out by teachers' colleges and departments of education. Innumerable studies over the years have shown that the kinds of college students who seek degrees in education are among the least qualified academically.

The problem is not simply that such people are unlikely to be capable of teaching the kinds of intellectual rigor that they themselves do not possess. That is unlikely even to be high on their priority list, if it is on the list at all.

The public schools' enormous preoccupation with maintaining the "self-esteem" of mediocre and sub-standard students, as well as educators' hostility to any form of ability-grouping, are perfectly understandable when these educators are themselves representatives of mediocrity and worse. It is unrealistic to expect such people to treasure high-ability students, much less to know how to develop such ability, or to prepare or guide its future development.

One of the strongest arguments for term limits is that the supply of people who want a career in politics is different from the supply of people willing to take a few years out from their regular careers to perform a public service. One of the strongest arguments for school choice and for ending tenure is that the public schools need

competition from a different supply of people who were not filtered
through education courses that are an abomination to anyone with a
first-rate mind.

Economics is not the only field where we need to look at the
supply side.

REFLECTIONS ON
TERM LIMITS

THE REFLECTING POOL between the Washington Monument and the
Lincoln Memorial may be the only thing in Washington that is reflecting. Preoccupation with the never-ending task of political fund-
raising, fighting daily brushfires, and trying to put the right spin on
the crisis du jour leaves very little time for the nation's political leaders to step back and contemplate deeper and enduring questions amid
the swirl of events and rhetoric.

Reflection is not a luxury but a prime necessity. Anyone who has
ever done anything as mundane as looking for a house knows how
much time and thought goes into weighing one place against another
and both against the bank account, not to mention the conflicting demands of getting to work, getting the children in a good school and
many other considerations.

Imagine if in one year you had to decide—and vote on—complex
environmental issues, foreign policy around the world, racial issues
at home, military defense, judicial appointments, and regulating public utilities, pharmaceutical drugs, the stock market and the safety of
mines, airports, food and vaccines. Even if we arbitrarily assume that
none of these things is any more complicated than buying a house,

how many people could handle all the problems of buying a house ten times in one year?

Worse yet, these national and international issues are not the sole—or even the main—business of those in Congress or the White House. Their main business is getting re-elected. That is also the main business of those who work for them, even though theoretically these staffers and appointees work for the country and certainly are paid by the taxpayers.

One of the strongest cases for term limits is that a one-term rule would free up a major block of time, and eliminate a major conflict-of-interest, among elected officials and their staffs, by eliminating their overwhelming preoccupation with getting re-elected. Those advocates of term limits who wish merely to restrict the number of terms forfeit much of this advantage for, if three terms are allowed for a Congressman, then in two-thirds of those terms the Congressman and his staff will still be preoccupied with re-election.

If the fear is that two years is too short a time for a member of the House of Representatives to get the lay of the land and become an effective legislator, then instead of allowing three two-year terms, one six-year term could be established. The point is to get people focussed on national concerns, not their own re-election.

Those who fear that we would lose the great "expertise" that members of Congress develop after years of dealing with certain issues fail to see that much of that expertise is in the arts of packaging, log-rolling, creative accounting and other forms of deception. Those who dominate the national political scene—and often the local scene, as well—are experts only in the law and in political machinations.

Genuine experts in particular fields seldom have either the incentive or the political talents to get elected to public office. A leading surgeon, engineer, corporate executive, scientist or financial consultant earns far more than the salary of any public official in Washington. What incentive is there for someone like this to sacrifice his family's present wellbeing and future security, unless he is so driven by the desire for power that any sacrifice seems worth it?

Anyone with such a craving for power is the last person to trust with power.

One of the greatest economy moves we could make would be to pay every member of Congress a million dollars a year, but with no perks and no pension. Paying this salary to each member of Congress for the entire 21st century would cost less than running the Department of Agriculture for one year.

This would pay for itself many times over because many government agencies and programs could be eliminated by a Congress not concerned with raising campaign money from special interests that benefit from bureaucracies ostensibly set up to serve the public.

With such a salary, people who are at the top of many fields could afford to spend one term in Washington performing a civic duty without sacrificing their families—and without any prospect that this could be a career from which they could retire with a pension.

The absence of perks would emphasize that they were not little tin gods but simply citizens temporarily serving in government. They could also bring some real expertise to Washington, expertise in something besides politics.

THE CENTURY OF THE INTELLECTUAL

THE TWENTIETH CENTURY HAS BEEN the century of the intellectual—and nowhere more so than in politics.

The two leading totalitarian regimes of this century, Nazi Germany and the Soviet Union, were created by writers and talkers: Adolf Hitler and V. I. Lenin. Hitler's *Mein Kampf,* and Lenin's *Imperialism* and other writings, were what put them on the map. The quality of their writings, in terms of logic or evidence, may have been shabby beyond belief. But these were masterpieces of propaganda.

Lenin's tracts rescued Marxism from the utter failures of its predictions and provided a whole new world vision, in which his political enemies were cast as international arch-villains, and Lenin's own followers as heroic agents of destiny.

Marxist-Leninist tracts like *Imperialism* gave comprehensive, dramatic and bitter explanations of the world's ills and discontents. Any sophomore could find in them the master keys to history, without the drudgery of having to know the facts or cope with the complexities of reality.

Hitler likewise created his own universe of the mind, peopled by whole races assigned their disparate roles in the grand scheme of history, and made titans or devils according to one man's imagination. Drivel? Yes. Powerfully effective? Also yes.

Some might say that these were pseudo-intellectuals or even anti-intellectuals, in terms of the quality of their reasoning or their use of evidence. But being an intellectual is an occupation, and the quality of their work does not change their occupation. A bad surgeon is still a surgeon—a deadly menace to the unsuspecting, but a surgeon nonetheless.

Being intellectuals was not an incidental part of the political careers of twentieth century dictators like Lenin, Hitler, or Mao. Their writings and sayings were the key instruments of their rise to power, just as military prowess was the key to Napoleon's. Moreover, their appeal was not just to the gullible masses, but to other intellectuals, including scholars, literary giants, and others with impeccable credentials in the world of ideas.

If totalitarianism was the ugly beast of twentieth century politics, its beauty was admired by the likes of George Bernard Shaw and Thorstein Veblen, and its apologists ranged from Pulitzer Prize-winning journalist Walter Duranty of the *New York Times* to whole armies of fellow-travelers in the media and academic world of their time.

The pilgrimages of intellectuals to the lands of the dictators—to Stalinist Russia, Maoist China, or Castro's Cuba—have been among the amazing stories of this century, as eminent scholars and literary figures have come back to gush over the "progress" of tyrannies whose own people were making desperate escapes whenever they could.

In short, totalitarianism has been an intellectual phenomenon. It appealed to the same susceptibilities of intellectuals as other crusades that have seized the imagination of the educated and the articulate— so-called "thinking people"—such as the eugenics movement in the early part of the century and, later, apocalyptic environmentalism demanding Draconian regulations.

What all these movements have in common is a sense of a revelation grasped only by the anointed, but a revelation that needs to be imposed on the benighted masses for their own good. Could anything be more of an ego trip, or more in keeping with intellectuals' exalted view of themselves, or their resentment at seeing wealth and power in the hands of lesser beings?

Nothing so mundane as mere evidence can be allowed to threaten a vision so deeply satisfying. People who escaped from totalitarian paradises, and who told tales of the horrors there, were dismissed as political enemies spreading lies.

Where the facts were too blatant to deny, the explanation was that these were "growing pains" of a new society or "local excesses," and we were reminded that "you can't make an omelette without breaking eggs." The fatal talent of the intelligentsia is facility with words—and a blindness to the fact that reality is not nearly so malleable as language.

Only after the official archives were opened in the last days of the Soviet Union did the unthinkable horrors of an evil empire become undeniable. Yes, there was a deliberately engineered famine in the Ukraine under Stalin—and its victims exceeded even the horrifying estimates in Robert Conquest's classic study of the subject. Yes, the Soviets carried out a mass murder of Polish military officers and—we learned more recently—the execution of American prisoners from as far back as World War II, when we were supposedly "allies."

The past is irrevocable, but many of the factors behind its tragedies are still at work in the present, and are a danger to the future. The issues change—eugenics is not environmentalism—but the dogmatism and the ego behind the dogmatism are the same.

CLOSET HUMANITARIANS

STAUNCH FREE-MARKET ECONOMIST though he is, Professor Walter Williams has admitted that his own household operates on the principle of communism: "From each according to his ability, to each according to his needs."

Although Professor Williams has publicly denounced the very idea that the government should take a dime of his money and give it to anyone else, in his private life he has given both money and time to all sorts of people.

Adam Smith himself, patron saint of laissez-faire economics, was discovered after his death to have secretly made many charitable contributions, much beyond what would have been expected from his financial situation. He also spent much time helping a blind young man to prepare for an intellectual career.

The late Professor Friedrich Hayek, another giant in the history of free market economics, argued that we are all believers in altruistic tribal values in our private lives—and that socialism is essentially the belief that these values can be applied politically to a complex economy.

In other words, we are all closet socialists at heart, though some of us believe that it would be disastrous for a whole society to come out of the closet and try to apply these primitive tribal values through a political bureaucracy in a modern economy and mass society.

Still, these tribal ideals continue to have a powerful influence today—and all across the political spectrum. Die-hard conservatives are busy redistributing their own incomes while they denounce the very idea of a redistribution of income. The rise of conservative think tanks all across the United States and as far away as Australia owes much to the generosity of these people.

Despite those who equate free-market economics with "greed," the heyday of laissez-faire economics in the 19th century also saw an unprecedented outpouring of private philanthropy. Moreover the "materialistic" Americans are unique in the many academic, medical and other institutions founded and sustained with private, voluntary contributions. These contributions accelerated to another all-time high during the 1980s, the "decade of greed," according to the political left.

Words like "compassion" are used by those on the left as if such words and such thoughts were their copyrighted private property. Yet there is not a speck of evidence that compassion is any more common in one part of the political spectrum than another.

At various junctures in history, liberals, socialists and others on the left have taken the lead in particular humanitarian crusades. The civil rights efforts of the 1950s and 1960s are an obvious example. But it is equally true that, at other junctures, conservatives have championed humanitarian causes.

One of the most remarkable humanitarian causes in history was the crusade to abolish slavery around the world. It is seldom even discussed today how this inhuman institution, which existed on all continents and lasted for thousands of years, was destroyed over most of the planet within a period of about one century.

It all began with a small group of very conservative religious people in England. Had the phrase "the religious right" existed at that time, it would certainly have applied to them. Rush Limbaugh would be to the left of these people.

William Wilberforce was the leader of this group, which was known as the Clapham sect because they often met at the Clapham estate of Henry Thornton, a staid and wealthy banker and one of the landmark figures in the development of monetary economics.

Hard as it is to transport ourselves back to another time and another universe of the mind, we must realize that slavery was so widely accepted among peoples all over the planet that even an attempt to bring the international trade in human beings to a halt was considered Utopian, and the idea of abolishing slavery itself was considered out of the question.

Wilberforce and Thornton made the abolition of the international slave trade their objective—and after 20 years of repeated defeats in Parliament, they finally won, when a bill banning the international slave trade in the British Empire was passed in 1807.

Although this bill simply abolished the trading of slaves, it was in fact the beginning of the end of slavery itself around the world. The long campaign for abolition of the slave trade ignited a moral revulsion against slavery itself that spread throughout Western civilization, and the spread of European imperialism led to the abolition of slavery in many non-Western societies as well.

There is no need to attempt the impossible task of determining whether people of one political persuasion rather than another have done more humanitarian things, especially if judged by results rather than intentions. The real question is how many of our humanitarian instincts can be applied politically in the world of today without creating more disasters.

THE SURVIVAL OF THE LEFT

BIOLOGISTS EXPLAIN HOW ORGANISMS ADAPT to their physical environment, but ideologues also adapt to their social environment. The most fundamental fact about the ideas of the political left is that they do not work. Therefore we should not be surprised to find the left concentrated in institutions where ideas do not have to work in order to survive.

The academic world is the natural habitat of half-baked ideas, except for those fields in which there are decisive tests, such as science, mathematics, engineering, medicine—and athletics. In all these fields, in their differing ways, there comes a time when you must either put up or shut up. It should not be surprising that all of these fields are notable exceptions to the complete domination of the left on campuses across the country.

In the humanities, for example, the test of deconstructionism is not whether it can produce any tangible results but whether it remains in vogue. So long as it does, professors skilled in its verbal sleight-of-hand can expect to continue to receive six-figure salaries.

You might think that the collapse of communism throughout Eastern Europe would be considered a decisive failure for Marxism, but academic Marxists in America are utterly undaunted. Their paychecks and their tenure are unaffected. Their theories continue to flourish in the classrooms and their journals continue to litter the library shelves.

Socialism in general has a record of failure so blatant that only an intellectual could ignore or evade it. Even countries that were once more prosperous than their neighbors have found themselves much poorer than their neighbors after just one generation of socialistic policies. Whether these neighboring countries were Ghana and the Ivory Coast or Burma and Thailand, it has been the same story around the world.

Nor is economic failure the worst of it. The millions slaughtered by Stalin, Mao and Pol Pot for political reasons are an even grimmer reality.

People who live and work in a world where there is a business bottom line, an athletic scoreboard, a military battlefield or life-and-death surgery may find it hard to fully appreciate the difference between that kind of world and one in which the only decisive test is whether your colleagues like what you are saying.

Academia is only one of the places where wholly subjective criteria rule—and where leftists predominate. Endowed institutions such as foundations and museums likewise often face no test other than what like-minded people find "exciting" and what enables those who run these institutions to get the heady feeling that they are "making a difference." The same is true of cultural institutions supported involuntarily by the taxpayers, such as the Smithsonian or the National Endowments for the Arts and the Humanities.

Taxpayer-supported "public" radio and television are similarly insulated from reality and similarly dominated by the left, not only in the United States but in other countries as well. All the nostrums of the left that have brought hunger to millions in countries which used to have surplus food to export, all the pretty words and ugly realities that have caused millions more to flee the lands of their birth, these nostrums live on in public television—much like old classic movies with familiar lines that the audience of aficionados can recite along with the characters on the screen.

These endowed and insulated institutions, often full of contempt for the values of American society and Western civilization, are not the only bastions of the left counter-culture. So are Hollywood and Broadway. Although show biz faces the financial need to get an audience, the truth of what they portray is hardly crucial. If they can make it punchy and sexy, then those who complain about historical inaccuracies and ideological bias can be dismissed as irrelevant pedants.

Why are leftists able to crowd out other kinds of people from these places? Because those who are willing to subject themselves to the test of reality, whether as a businessman in the marketplace or as a surgeon in an operating room, have many other places in which to work and live. They do not need special sheltered niches in which to hide and to cherish their precious notions.

Darwinian adaptation to environment applies not only to nature but also to society. Just as you don't find eagles living in the ocean or fish living on mountain tops, so you don't find leftists concentrated where their ideas have to stand the test of performance.

GAYS IN THE MILITARY

THE ISSUE OF GAYS IN THE MILITARY gives the anointed an opportunity to play their favorite role as enlightened Olympians lecturing the benighted masses.

"The issue is bigotry," according to *New York Times* columnist Anthony Lewis. In a *Los Angeles Times* column, Richard Rodriguez pictures those who disagree with him on this issue as "insecure heterosexual males," as "bald and bellied politicians," and pictures the Joint Chiefs of Staff as "looking like Victorian fathers."

Although people in the media make a lot of noise about "the public's right to know," that seldom includes the right to know the reasons behind opposition to something that the media believe in. It is extremely doubtful that most media will present the reasons on both sides of the issue of gays in the military. It would be completely out of character if they did.

Whatever the issue, a concern that is important to the media is called "a matter of principle," but a concern that is important to those on the other side is called "an emotional issue." Apparently only the anointed have reasons and principles. Others just have emotional reactions, psychological hang-ups, and pot bellies.

Even where there is the pretense of presenting both sides, often that means presenting the reasons of one side and the anger of the other.

If we are serious about any issue, let us begin with the reality. The most fundamental reality about the military is that it is in a life-and-death business, on which the life and death of nations, as well as individuals, depends. We are not discussing an abstract issue around a seminar table.

When military units perform better or worse, it means not only the difference between victory and defeat, but also the difference between life and death for the people in those units.

The military performance that matters is the performance of organizations, not the performances of particular individuals—despite all the talk about how particular gays have had exemplary records in military service. Even in something much less important, like sports, everyone understands that it is teams which win or lose—and that a team that works well together often defeats a team with more individual stars.

The individual records of individual gays that are being paraded in the media make clever talking points, as do analogies to the situation of blacks in the military in times past. But talking points and analogies are suggestive at best, and certainly not decisive when considering a life and death organization.

If we are not going to be serious about life and death, when are we going to be serious?

The serious question is how the official acceptance of homosexuality will affect the performance of military units as a whole. That same question must be answered as to the role of women in the military, or the role of draftees, for that matter. It is not a question of how individuals perform their tasks individually.

If we are serious, then we are talking about people living together in barracks and tents, not performing separate tasks in a nine to five job. If we are serious, then we are talking about the rigid subordination inherent in military organizations for thousands of years—and about what that means when there are sexual affinities among military personnel of different ranks.

The potential for sexual harassment is only one of the problems. Wholly voluntary sexual relations, whether among gays or between men and women, affect the morale of others, when those others must wonder about favoritism, and especially about favoritism in combat.

Military morale is an intangible, but it is one of those intangibles without which the tangibles do not work.

What of recruitment for an all-volunteer military service, when potential recruits know that this means sleeping in barracks and tents with homosexuals? What about the likelihood that military bases, like other concentrations of young males such as colleges, will become magnets for civilian homosexuals?

This has already happened at various colleges and universities around the country. Complaints have come from men who find that using the toilets means being either solicited or being witnesses to homosexual activity.

Homosexual men have been attracted to the toilets at the University of Florida from as far as 40 miles away. This university, as well as Dartmouth, Georgetown, and the University of California at San Diego, have been forced to install stainless steel panels between toilet stalls to prevent the drilling of holes in the walls for homosexual activity.

The issue is not whether all homosexuals, or even most homosexuals, do such things. The question is whether such activity is going to become a problem if homosexuality becomes as accepted in the military as it has become on many college campuses.

These are only some of the arguments and some of the facts that the public will not be given a "right to know" in most of the media.

THE CHICKEN LITTLE MEDIA

VIRTUALLY EVERY NEWS PROGRAM seemed to feature the recent demonstration about "battered women" held on the Washington mall and sponsored by the radical feminists of the National Organization for Women. The propaganda put out by this group of activists was reported as "news," without a skeptical word being spoken, much less someone with different views being allowed to criticize some of the sweeping claims and wild rhetoric.

It is not that anyone is in favor of battering women. But there are still some people left who are in favor of the truth.

In a country of a quarter of a billion people, there are indeed examples of battered wives. There are also battered husbands, battered bachelors and battered women living in lesbian relationships. Justice Department data show more than a million cases of aggravated assault on men annually and less than half that number of aggravated assaults on women.

Shrill activists in the feminist movement love to quote statistics that lump together everything from spats to homicide. For example, some statistics count a husband's stomping out of the room as "emotional abuse." One poll showed that about a third of all husbands do that at some point during the year—as compared to 2 percent who actually physically assault their wives. How many wives stomp out of the room is apparently not known.

Husbands who merely grab their wives during an argument—perhaps to keep her from stomping out of the room—are counted in some statistics on physical assault. However, statistics which deal with genuine violence usually turn up numbers less than one-tenth of the numbers that are being thrown around in the media by activists with axes to grind.

The more militant feminists don't even bother to twist facts. They just make them up. A few years ago, it was widely reported that great numbers of wives were battered on Super Bowl Sunday, when the men were supposedly feeling especially macho.

The media ate it up. Only after a few brave souls dared to ask for the source of this information about Super Bowl Sunday did the story start to unravel and it became apparent that this whole thing was made up.

It is not enough for us to discover belatedly that we have been lied to. It is far more important that we remember who the liars are and not be so gullible next time.

We also need to realize that the media love stories that undermine the family, traditional values and everything else that stands in the way of the liberal agenda.

On March 27, 1991, for example, Dan Rather said on the CBS Evening News that a "startling number of American children are in danger of starving" because "one out of eight American children is going hungry tonight."

Where did he get those numbers? From a group of activists. And where did the activists get the numbers? From a survey they conducted that asked this question:

"Thinking about the past 12 months, did you ever rely on a limited number of foods to feed your children because you were running out of money to buy food for a meal?"

The question was not abut whether the child went hungry, much less faced "starvation." It was about whether the variety—not amount—of food was less than it would have been if more money had been available. In other words, did you ever get burgers and fries when you would have preferred to serve a real meal?

The question was not about whether this happened every night, or even regularly, but whether it happened at all, at any time during the previous year. Because one out of eight parents said that it did, this became transformed into one out of eight American children being "hungry"—and "tonight," with "starvation" looming in the background.

Actual examinations of flesh-and-blood human beings by the Centers for Disease Control turned up no indication of malnutrition among Americans at any income level. Low-income women were in fact more likely to be obese.

Although the media love to wrap themselves in the mantle of "concern," with the aura of morality radiating in the background, the philosopher Pascal said that the first moral duty is to think clearly. Our media would be doing well to think at all, instead of echoing whatever the politically correct activists feed them.

Most of what the activists feed them is the real junk food. Our whole society could become malnourished from an inadequate supply of the truth.

Networks that pay anchormen millions of dollars can surely afford to hire a few statisticians to check the flow of fraudulent numbers coming in to them. Or is moral posturing considered a substitute for clear thinking?

MUSH, CANT AND IMMIGRATION

IMMIGRATION IS ONE OF A GROWING number of issues that cannot be discussed rationally. Mush and cant are the standard ingredients in any debate on the subject. Some examples:

"We are a nation of immigrants."

"Diversity is our strength."

"Criticism of immigration is racist."

None of these statements is an argument. Each is a way of not making an argument, while pretending to do so.

Of course we are a nation of immigrants. So are most other nations. The English are not the indigenous people of England, the Turks are not the indigenous people of Turkey and the Malays are not the indigenous people of Malaysia. But so what?

The fact that immigrants were once valuable additions to the country does not mean that the same thing may be arbitrarily assumed today, any more than the fact that horses and buggies were once the best way to get around means that we should rely on them today.

If you want to make an argument for immigration, then make an argument for immigration. But don't waste everybody's time with lofty buzzwords.

One of the problems with discussing immigrants in general is that there is no such thing as an immigrant in general. Not only do they vary from one individual to another, whole categories of immigrants have very different histories, both in their respective homelands and in the United States.

Less than 5 percent of the immigrants from Britain or Germany go on welfare when they get here, but more than one fourth the immigrants from Vietnam go on welfare, as do nearly half of those from Cambodia. That compares to 14 percent among American blacks.

If making any distinction among immigrant groups is "racist," as the intelligentsia seem to think, then apparently the choice facing the country is to be racist or to be suckers who pay for anyone who wants to come here and live off the American taxpayers. Nothing will promote racism more than a choice like that.

What about that wonderful "diversity" we hear so many rhapsodies about?

You want diversity? They have diversity in Bosnia, in Somalia, in Rwanda and in various former Soviet republics where people are today slaughtering each other just for belonging to the "wrong" group.

We haven't reached that point yet, but give us time. Already polls are indicating that young whites and young blacks are more hostile to one another than are their elders. What does that say about the future? Throw in a few more groups, and lots of "leaders" and activists to hype their differences, and our future may not be a lot better than that of other "multicultural" and "diverse" nations.

Do immigrants contribute nothing? Of course they contribute something. Some immigrants—Albert Einstein and Edward Teller, for example—have undoubtedly saved tens of thousands of American lives by making this the first nuclear nation. That not only brought World War II to an end without leaving the beaches of Japan strewn with the bodies of American soldiers, it made any new Pearl Harbor against the United States a suicidal gamble for any other country.

Some immigrants come here with more of the traditional American values of work and family than many of the current generation of Americans. Many come here wanting nothing more than to become Americans. But many of the morally anointed intelligentsia want them to stay foreign in culture and alienated from the values of the country.

To a large segment of the intelligentsia, immigration is just one more stage on which to engage in moral preening, showing off their own wonderful specialness compared to the grubby masses. They treat immigration to the United States as if it were a civil right of foreigners around the world and regard any thought of controlling our own borders in the interest of the people who live here as mean-spirited.

One of the few books to challenge this vision of the anointed is the recently published *Alien Nation* by Peter Brimelow. This book has its flaws, but it is one of the few opportunities to see what arguments can be made against immigration.

Brimelow points out, for example, that diseases once virtually extinct in the United States, such as tuberculosis, leprosy and measles, have now been introduced again by immigrants from the Third World. Crime rates are also very high among some immigrant groups.

Anyone who wants to see arguments on the other side can read any of a number of pro-immigration books or essays by Julian Simon. The point here is that the whole subject of immigration policy has been beset with taboos for too long.

All sorts of rational arguments can be made for or against immigration. It is just that very few are. Among the questions that need to be addressed are: How many and from where?

PHONEY ARGUMENTS FOR QUOTAS

AFTER MORE THAN A QUARTER of a century of listening to arguments in favor of affirmative action, I have finally realized that there are no arguments in favor of affirmative action. There are only ploys, evasions and emotional rhetoric.

The latest ploy is to say that "angry white men" are the reason for recent efforts to repeal group preferences and quotas. In fact, polls have repeatedly shown that no segment of American society is in favor of such things when they are called by their right names. Moreover, a recent poll showed that, while 61 percent of white males were against affirmative action, so are 65 percent of non-white males.

Having reduced the issue from one of principle to one of emotion, advocates of affirmative action then pose the question: Would these "angry white males" be willing to "trade places" with those whom they say receive preferential treatment? It is the kind of sound-bite cleverness that plays so well in the media.

First of all, most people don't want to be somebody else, simply because they are too used to being themselves. But the more fundamental falseness of the assumptions behind this question is that nothing more is at stake than a set of arbitrary advantages.

This blithely ignores centuries of struggle, sacrifice and bloodshed to get laws that apply to everyone alike. The civil rights movement of the 1950s and 1960s was a late phase of that long struggle, which went on for centuries in England before it began in America. The civil rights movement succeeded in great part because it was seen as a continuation of that historic fight for that principle.

Now everything is suddenly to be reduced to the question of whose ox is gored and whose emotions are to be appeased.

A larger confusion is often involved as well. It may undoubtedly be "unfair" in some cosmic sense that all the skills, all the experience, all the drives and behavior patterns that make for achievement are not equally distributed to all groups everywhere. But they never have been.

All groups trail the long shadow of their history behind them. Groups whose cultures developed in industrial, scientific and commercial environments are more likely to grow up oriented toward the kinds of things that are useful in industrial, scientific and commercial activities.

This is not a racial difference. The history of northwestern Europeans has contrasted with the history of southeastern Europeans for centuries—not only in Europe, but wherever immigrants from these two parts of the same continent have competed with one another overseas. Nor have all Asians been the same as other Asians or all Africans the same as other Africans.

The idea that all groups bring the same human capital to the marketplace or to the schoolroom is one of those romantic but childishly silly ideas that flies in the face of massive evidence to the contrary from around the world. It is taken seriously only because so many of the intelligentsia adopt it in their groupthink and newspeak.

The cultural history of coastal peoples has been different from the history of peoples in the interior hinterlands and the mountains, even when they were all racially identical. They could pass on the same genes to the next generation without passing on the same cultures, the same skills, the same aspirations. No one who believes in cause and effect should be surprised that the results are also different.

The question is: What are we going to do about it?

Is government policy going to say that skills, experience, etc., do not matter? Or is anyone hopelessly optimistic enough to think that these factors in success can be equalized by social programs, within any time period that is politically relevant?

Are we to play make-believe for another generation or another century and say that demographic "representation" takes precedence over getting the job done? Are we to indulge in absolute fantasy and say that statistical "diversity" promotes better intergroup relations, shutting our eyes tight against blatant evidence that it is poisoning people against one another?

Are we to pretend that the roles of wife and mother do not make huge demands on time and on energy, leaving less of both for other things? As one who was a single parent for years between marriages, I can tell you that raising a child is not a spare time activity. There is no mystery to me as to why women who take on these roles do not have the same track record in the economy as most men who don't.

But are we to blame the realities of life on employers, on government, on "society"? Here as elsewhere, what intellectuals are fundamentally revolting against is the fact that the universe was not built to their specifications.

Perhaps they should launch a class-action lawsuit—"Harvard and Berkeley et al versus the Almighty." They would certainly get a sympathetic hearing in the Supreme Court.

RIP VAN WASHINGTON

"THIS IS S. O. TERRICK, REPORTING for your eyewitness news team. We have an amazing story from an amazing guest tonight. Here he is—Rip Van Washington. Thank you for being here with us tonight, Mr. Van Washington."

"Thank you. I am glad to be here."

"Glad to be awake, too, I imagine."

"Yes."

"Ladies and gentlemen, Mr. Van Washington fell asleep listening to a political speech back in 1974—and just woke up today."

"Yes, I have a lot of catching up to do. When I fell asleep in 1974, we had a tricky President whom no one trusted. I am sure he must be gone by now, so that problem should be behind us."

"Well, that particular President is gone, but I'm not sure the problem is behind us."

"Back in 1974, we were just getting out of the quagmire in Vietnam. It was so awful that I am sure we are never getting into anything like that again."

"I'm not so sure about that either, Mr. Van Washington."

"You mean the right-wing hawks are trying to get us into another quagmire?"

"Actually, it's the left-wing hawks this time. They are for intervention in Haiti, in Bosnia . . . "

"Left-wing hawks! Things have really changed in 20 years."

"Oh, yes. In fact 'change' is one of the big political buzzwords of our times."

"Really? You mean they no longer believe in all that welfare state stuff?"

"Well, no, that's not what they mean by change."

"You mean that people no longer talk about the 'root causes' of crime?"

"Well, actually they still do. And it still doesn't get us anywhere."

"Do you mean the government is no longer spending hundreds of billions of dollars?"

"Actually they are spending more than ever. Trillion is the word nowadays."

"Then what has changed?"

"It's kind of hard to explain, Mr. Van Washington. May I call you Rip?"

"Please do."

"Well, Rip, one of the changes, for example, is that the purpose of the current welfare reform proposals is to 'end welfare as we know it'."

"You mean like Lyndon Johnson's saying that 'the days of the dole are numbered' when the war on poverty programs began? That was ten years old when I fell asleep."

"All right, let me try another example of 'change.' The government wants to expand its role in health care."

"You mean like it did with Medicare?"

"Yeah but this new program is supposed to make things better, not create a lot of problems and have runaway costs like Medicare."

"Medicare was supposed to make things better. As for costs, they were already starting to go up when I fell asleep. What's happened since then?"

"They have now shot up out of sight."

"So where's the 'change' that everyone is talking about?"

"All right. Let me try again. Today the President's wife is very vocal on public issues and exercises influence on policy."

"You mean like Eleanor Roosevelt? Or like the harem favorites in the Ottoman Empire?"

"Mr. Van Washington, this is turning out to be harder to explain than I thought. But just bear with me. For example, the government wants to improve American education by spending more money on it—'Investing' in education is what they call it."

"The government started doing that back in the 1960s—and they called it 'investment' then. That's when test scores started going down. Incidentally, have they gotten back up again to where they were back in the 1960s?"

"No. In fact, we hit a new all-time low on verbal scores on the Scholastic Aptitude Test in 1991."

"This is all very confusing."

"I know it must be, Rip. Here, have a glass of water. We'll get you something stronger after the show."

"Is there no hope that our children's test scores will go up again?"

"Yes there is, actually. The people who produce the SAT have changed the norms, so the new scores will be higher. The kids may not know any more, but the scores will be higher."

"Oh, no."

"Rip, you look a little ill. Is anything wrong?"

"No, I'm just feeling sleepy again."

COMING FROM BEHIND

IT IS NOT UNUSUAL FOR TEAMS in various sports to come from behind. But, in order to do that, you first have to recognize that you are behind and play accordingly. Too many conservatives, in the post-1994 election euphoria, imagined that they were ahead. But that election was like hitting a home run with the bases loaded when you are ten runs behind. It is a good start, but only a start.

The education of the next generation, from the kindergarten to the graduate school, is firmly in the hands of the political left. Moreover, unlike many conservatives, the countercultural left understands that they are in a war for the soul of this country. They do not observe any Marquis of Queensberry rules in that war. They do not hesitate to apply ideological litmus tests to everything from faculty hiring to the rewriting of history.

Nor do they hesitate to use everything from grades to the student disciplinary process, including expulsion, to punish students who say something politically incorrect. Speech codes on elite college campuses across the country are vaguely worded, not because there is no one capable of plain English, but because vagueness serves the twin purposes of intimidation and allowing the authors of these codes to deny intimidation.

Studies documenting the lopsided liberal-left political views of the media have appeared so often over so many years that this should not be in any doubt, though here too there are lofty ways of denying or evading this plain fact. However, it is not simply the personal opinions of reporters but the extent to which they are willing to slant the news in support of those opinions which is a key to the culture wars of our time. N.B.C.'s rigged "test" of a truck's gas tank, with explosives secretly planted to make it blow up on camera, is a classic example of this mindset—and its effects on journalistic ethics.

Joseph A. Schumpeter once said that the first thing a man will do for his ideals is lie. The ideologues of academe are no exception. Moreover, even scholars caught lying may be excused if it was in "a good cause" as seen by the left. In one example a few years ago, a historian who exposed and documented fraud by another historian seeking to promote leftist conclusions was denounced by many other academics for jeopardizing a young scholar's career, even though no one challenged the accuracy of the exposé.

The American Library Association sponsors an annual—and fraudulent—"Banned Books Week" in which "banned books" are defined and counted to include books that anybody can buy anywhere and which the government itself often buys by the thousands. Anyone who objects to school books which graphically portray gang rapes to classes of ten-year-olds, or which systematically ridicule religion, or which show pictures of naked adults engaging in various homosexual acts, is accused of "censorship" for opposing the brainwashing of children behind their parent's backs.

Professional associations of all sorts have in recent years become politicized by the left. The National Education Association routinely votes "politically correct" resolutions on non-educational issues ranging from immigration to environmentalism. The American Bar Association, the Modern Language Association, and other professional organizations have likewise succumbed to ideological crusades, even at the expense of professional integrity.

Above all, the political left understands the crucial importance of institutionalizing whatever political advantages they have at the moment, so that these advantages will survive long after that moment. Thus New Deal agencies created during the Great Depression of the 1930s are still alive—and growing—in the 1990s. Conservatives seem to have no corresponding awareness of a need to get rid of such programs root and branch.

Despite a majority in both houses of Congress, the Republicans have not been willing to get rid of even such small agencies as the National Endowment for the Humanities or the Legal Services Corporation, both of which have long been shock troops for the counterculture. Budget cuts for such entrenched and determined opponents of the basic values of this country are like running a lawn mower over crabgrass. If you are not prepared to root it out, you are just wasting your time and kidding yourself.

Despite the economic prosperity of the country, the indicators of social degeneracy are all around us—violent crime rates and rates of teenage pregnancy both several times higher than they were within living memory being just one example. Students' ignorance and inability to think, in even our best schools and colleges, means that they are ripe prey for demagogues—with the future of this country being correspondingly jeopardized.

We can still come from behind in the bottom of the ninth—but only if we realize that we are behind and that it is the bottom of the ninth.

MORE THAN MEETS THE EYE

LAST YEAR, AFTER OUR HOME began to look more and more like an unkempt library with a bed and kitchen, my wife decided that we needed to have someone build extensions to give us more room. However, the idea of remodeling was so appalling that I decided that what we needed was another house.

Since the new place needed some work too, I became acquainted with carpenters, electricians, furnace experts, carpet installers and painters. At first, I couldn't see the need for all the work that ended up getting done. The paint looked all right to me, for example, but the painter patiently took me for a walk around the outside of the house, pointing out things that ranged from unsightly to alarming.

It was the same story with the carpenters, the furnace people and others. There was always ten times more than met the eye the first time—but of course their eyes had seen such things many times before.

This experience reinforced what I should have known all along—that even an educated person is ignorant outside a narrow range of subjects and even an intelligent person is shallow on most of the things that make up the vast spectrum of human activities. Too many people fail to understand this reality, including many people in Washington, the media and academia.

That the President of the United States wanted to take on such tasks of settling the baseball strike, taking over the nation's health care system and solving problems that have plagued the Balkans for centuries is one sign of a mind which refuses to recognize its own inherent limitations. The modern welfare state and judicial activism are monuments to the same hubris—and the social degeneracy and the breakdown of law and order which have followed are painful reminders of ancient warnings about the consequences of hubris.

If someone with a Ph.D. can't even tell if a house needs painting, how are Congressmen, judges, and bureaucrats going to tell millions of other people how to run their businesses, raise their own children, or do the thousands of other things that people with first-hand knowledge understand far better than any politician in Washington or any theorist in academia?

While we often complain about particular government policies or particular court decisions, often the more fundamental problem is that politicians and judges tried to deal with things for which they lacked either the depth of knowledge required or the means (or will) to monitor their mistakes and correct them.

The sheer volume of annual legislation on such highly disparate things as military strategy, the labyrinthine educational system, complex environmental issues, racial cross-currents, and a multi-trillion-dollar economy with global interactions, is a monument to Congressional arrogance. Too often the results are a monument to their incompetence.

Nowhere are presumptions of omnicompetence more pervasive than among federal judges. Judge Stanley Sporkin's recent rejection of a proposed consent decree between the Justice Department and the Microsoft Corporation was another example of the kind of judicial hubris that has turned our legal system into a shambles. Nowhere in his opinion does Judge Sporkin cite a single clear-cut provision of the law that Microsoft is even alleged to have violated. Instead, he declares that Microsoft's practice of announcing in advance software that it is still developing is "terribly bothersome to this court."

Are we living under laws that tell us in advance what we can and cannot do or are we supposed to guess what will turn out to be "bothersome" to some judge? The difference is the difference between "a government of laws and not of men" and judicial tyranny. Judge Sporkin's complaint that Microsoft is not behaving as a "mature" corporation is more of the same kind of ex post facto pronouncement from the bench.

The question is not what will happen to Microsoft, which can undoubtedly take care of itself. The question is what is happening to law in this country.

During the early centuries of the Ottoman Empire's conquest of the Balkans, the Christian peoples of that region became loyal subjects of the sultan, even though they were explicitly second-class under the Islamic laws of the realm. But at least they were living under law, not under the arbitrary caprices of Christian noblemen who had ruled them before the Ottoman conquest.

Within some limits, even bad law, unequal law and unjust law is preferred to arbitrary rule. Law, as such, has value—a value blithely thrown away by activist judges who are busy taking on the role of philosopher-king, for which they have no more qualifications than I have to be a painter.

LOGIC TAKES ITS REVENGE

IF "FACTS ARE STUBBORN THINGS," logic is absolutely vengeful against those who ignore it. Many of today's festering racial problems are the logical consequences of notions accepted casually in the past, with little attempt to trace out their implications. For example, many who are pained by the growth of antisemitism among blacks have promoted ideas whose logical consequence is antisemitism, even though they had no such consequences in mind.

For decades now, it has been a central dogma of our political and legal institutions that statistical discrepancies between the "representation" of one group and another is evidence—sometimes virtually proof—of discrimination. In other words, the absence of an even representation implies sinister goings-on, whether it is in employment, college admissions, or the jailing of criminals. If machinations explain the difference between success and failure, then Jews must have been doing more than their share of machinations.

Jews have so many achievements and so much prominence in so many fields that it is hard to believe that there are fewer Jews in the entire world than there are Kazakhs or Sri Lankans. Like most other groups in countries around the world, Jews are not randomly distributed in various fields of endeavor, but tend to be concentrated in some fields far more so than others. If fields where men usually outnumber women are called "male-dominated," why is it surprising that fields in which Jews are particularly prominent are said to be "dominated" by Jews?

These fields may in fact be wide open to any Gentiles who can cut the mustard, just as basketball is wide open to any white players with the ability to compete against Charles Barkley et al. The reality, however, is that special skills and talents are seldom randomly distributed, despite our social dogmas.

But if you buy the logic of affirmative action, you buy the logic of antisemitism. Moral aversions to antisemitism, especially in the wake of the Nazi Holocaust, prevents most people from following the inner logic of their argument. But do not be surprised that there are some who do.

At colleges all across this country, antisemitic speakers are being brought onto campus with five-figure fees that are the least of the costs of their harangues. Moreover, this is done with university funds earmarked for minority benefits, in the name of "diversity," "multiculturalism," and other buzzwords that drive out thought the way bad money drives out good.

Most college administrators are not concerned about stopping this but about stopping the alumni and the public from finding out about it. These administrators are not necessarily antisemites themselves. They are instinctively following the path of least resistance. If found out, they will take refuge in another thoughtless buzzword—"censorship"—to explain why they not only tolerate but finance such hate-mongering.

The real reason they do it is that putting a stop to this lucrative bigotry can provoke outbursts of disruption from the militant elements of minority mini-establishments on campus, while Jewish students are very unlikely to riot if the antisemites give talks.

Antisemitism is only one of many areas in which logic takes its revenge. Many people are distressed that an attitude holds sway in

ghetto schools that doing well academically is "acting white"—
something to be avoided like the plague. But those who are distressed
often include people who have provided the logical underpinnings
for these self-destructive attitudes.

If differences in achievement are due only to differences in the
way "society" treats different groups, then why should black students knock themselves out on their school work, when Whitey is
just waiting in ambush to keep them from getting ahead anyway?
Liberals who have been pushing this line for decades should not be
surprised if these assumptions are now being followed out to their
logical conclusion.

Ironically, both affirmative action and the argument for genetic
inferiority of blacks use the same logic. They assume that statistical
results not explainable by obvious gross differences must be explainable by the underlying factor they prefer to believe in.

All this ignores the innumerable and powerful cultural influences
which direct some people's efforts in some directions and other people's efforts in others. Once, while teaching an all-black class at
Howard University, I asked them to imagine what would happen if a
black child in the middle of the ghetto were born with brain cells
identical to those with which Einstein entered the world.

There was much interesting speculation, but not one person in
that room thought that this child would grow up to be another Einstein. If he were born to a teenage mother in a gang-infested area, he
might be lucky to grow up at all—and he might well be one of those
conditioned to believe that putting his efforts into academic work
would be "acting white."

MODEST PROPOSALS

ONE OF THE GRAND FRAUDS of the political left is the notion that they have some sort of monopoly on "change"—that they are "progressive" while their adversaries oppose change or even want to go back to the past.

In reality, no one is opposed to generic "change," though some may oppose particular changes advocated by liberals and leftists. Many past and present figures regarded as "conservative" have in fact advocated radical changes.

Milton Friedman has advocated monetary policies radically different from anything followed by the Federal Reserve, today or in the past, and has advocated educational vouchers long before there were even limited or experimental vouchers. Robert H. Bork once advocated that courts declare the Robinson-Patman Act void for vagueness. On the last page of *The Wealth of Nations,* written in 1776, Adam Smith said that the British should let go of their colonies.

In order to try to follow, in a modest way, in such illustrious footsteps, let me suggest a few proposals for "change"—but outside the usual liberal-left framework.

None of our institutions is in more dire need of reform than our legal system in general and our criminal justice system in particular.

Judges, like politicians, ought to be subject to term limits, rather than have the lifetime appointments enjoyed by the federal judiciary. That might help stop them from acting like little tin gods who can expand the laws and the constitution to mean whatever they want them to mean.

A five- or ten-year term, at the end of a distinguished legal career, ought to be long enough for anyone to be trusted with the lives and liberties of his fellow-citizens. The knowledge that one's time on Olympus was limited, that one would have to return to the level of ordinary mortals on a fixed date, might be very salutary. More streamlined procedures for impeachments of judges who flagrantly misinterpret plainly-worded laws would also help.

Professional jurors are another reform that could help speed up the legal system and end its dangerous overload. It would do this in two different ways.

First of all, the process of choosing a jury to hear a particular case would not be the long, drawn-out process that it is today. The pool of potential jurors would already have been chosen by criteria designed to get knowledgeable, impartial people, capable of logical thinking and not easily swayed by appeals to emotions and prejudices. The jury for the particular case at hand would then be chosen by lot from this pool, not by attorneys jockeying for position.

What makes today's jury selection such a contest of ingenuity between opposing attorneys is that both are trying to get a jury which will not be impartial, but whose prejudices or emotional susceptibilities favor their particular clients. Not only the interests of a speedy trial, but also the interests of justice, favor dumping this gamesmanship in favor of an impartial process.

Once a professional and experienced jury was in place, there would also be less reason for attorneys to spend their time—and waste the court's time—on emotional appeals and attempts to confuse the issues.

In the area of economic policy, one of the simplest ways to cut back government spending would be to start at the top, by taking millionaires off the dole. A law or a constitutional amendment could simply state that no one whose income or net worth exceeded one million dollars was eligible to receive any transfer payments from the federal government.

Since so many recipients of agricultural subsidies have assets in excess of a million dollars, this would automatically chop billions of dollars out of the federal budget. Nor would the media be able to whip up sympathy for these "victims" of heartless budget-cutters, as they can when the cutbacks begin with welfare recipients.

Another modest proposal is that we have one branch of Congress elected nationally, at large. One of the reasons for so much porkbarrel spending is that "all politics is local politics," even when it takes place in Washington. As things stand now, there are only two nationally elected officials, the president and the vice-president.

If there were nationally-elected senators, for example, there would be someone to counter-balance the locally-oriented Congressmen whose prime incentive is to loot the national treasury for the folks back home. Since it is hard to envision existing senators voting themselves out of office, a third house of Congress might have to be created.

Are any of these proposals "practical" today? Of course not. None of the major reforms of the past were practical when they were first proposed. That is the reason for proposing them, to try to get people to start thinking about them.

PART IV
THE LEGAL SCENE

TAMPERING WITH THE CONSTITUTION

WHENEVER A NEW CONSTITUTIONAL AMENDMENT is proposed, the arguments against the particular policy are usually supplemented by the contention that we should not "tamper with the constitution."

Constantly changing the legal framework of a whole society is obviously not a good idea. Yet those who argue this way have often been not merely accepting but enthusiastic when judges have tampered with the constitution to have it mean things that no one ever dreamt that it meant before. In fact, many of the recent proposals for constitutional amendments have been attempts to restore previously understood meanings of that document.

Whatever the merits or demerits of policy arguments on each side in the abortion controversy, for example, this was never a constitutional issue until 1973—nearly two centuries after the constitution was written. The greatest legal minds in the history of the Supreme Court had never dreamed that the constitution mandated one policy or another on abortion. Headstrong lightweights like Justice Harry Blackmun then rushed in with the *Roe v. Wade* decision, where the likes of Holmes and Frankfurter feared to tread.

Cheers from the liberal galleries of the media and the law schools drowned out the question as to whether this was not tampering with the constitution. A "woman's right to do what she wants to with her own body" became an overwhelming cry. But government by overwhelming cries is the antithesis of constitutional law.

A constitutional democracy exists precisely so that people with different views can air those views and work out some resolution through the political processes. Nor need this be one uniform resolution throughout a large federal system. One size does not always fit all and some jurisdictions may reach different resolutions from others.

All this was short-circuited by the Supreme Court's *Roe v. Wade* decision, making abortion a "constitutional right," though no such right was ever written into the constitution. It was a judicial coup d'etat.

Issues ranging from capital punishment to nativity scenes at Christmas have likewise been removed from the democratic process by these judicial coups. Those who most vehemently reject "tampering with the constitution" through the amendment process established by the constitution itself have seldom, if ever, opposed judicial tampering. Indeed, they have cheered it on.

Legitimate concerns about tampering have been used disingenuously to try to leave tampering in the hands of those likely to support the policies favored by liberal ideology.

A similar fraudulence can be seen in the cries of horror as some of the liberal precedents of the Warren Court era have been scaled back in recent years. Precedents have suddenly become sacred to those who could scarcely contain their delight when the Warren Court overturned precedents that had stood for generations.

The requirements for a constitutional amendment—super majorities in Congress and among the state legislatures—are far more stringent than the verbal sleight-of-hand by which a handful of Supreme Court justices can "interpret" the words of the constitution to mean whatever their social vision dictates.

The recent Supreme Court decision striking down laws against term limits was a stark demonstration of constitutional "interpretation" as raw power in action—and hypocrisy in action, both on the part of the majority justices and of those in politics and the media who are opposed to both term limits and to constitutional amendments.

The constitution itself is remarkably clear and straightforward about what the states and the federal government can do. The Tenth Amendment says it all in one sentence: "The powers not delegated to the United States by the Constitution, nor prohibited by it to the States, are reserved to the States respectively, or to the people." In other words, the feds can do only what they are specifically authorized to do, but the states or the people can do whatever they are not specifically forbidden to do.

Supreme Court "interpretation": The states were never authorized to pass term limits, therefore it is unconstitutional for them to
do so. Are we talking tampering or are we talking tampering?

This decision, turning the Tenth Amendment upside down, was
possible only because the Court has been emboldened by acceptance
and acclaim for a long series of similar usurpations of power. The
time may be long overdue for term limits on judges.

QUOTAS ALIVE AND WELL

SOME OPPONENTS OF AFFIRMATIVE ACTION may have been cheered
by a federal case in Texas where the court ruled that the University
of Texas law school's special minority admissions program violated
the 14th Amendment's requirement of equal protection of the law.
However, quotas are still alive and well after this decision. Whether
the 14th Amendment is still alive and well is another question.

Four white students who applied to the law school at the University of Texas, and were turned down, sued because minority students with lesser credentials were admitted. They won the case—and
were awarded one dollar each in damages, as well as the right to apply again next year. If it were not for the honor of the thing, they
might as well have lost. The rule of law lost even bigger.

For those still naive enough to expect judges to follow the plain
words of the written law, federal district judge Sam Sparks disabused
them of this notion early in his opinion. Although the 14th Amendment guarantees "equal protection of the laws," Judge Sparks dismissed "a simplistic application" of these words. According to the
judge, "giving minority applicants a 'plus' is lawful." In other words,
some are more equal than others.

How does he reconcile this with the Constitution's requirement
of equal protection? By referring to a "tension that exists when the
individual rights of non-minorities come into conflict with programs designed to aid minorities." Tension is a much loftier word
than contradiction—and not as honest. Its practical effect is to allow
judges to pick and choose when they will apply the written law and
when they will not.

For the ordinary citizen, it means that there is no way to know in
advance what is and is not legal. Contrary to the Constitution's prohibition against ex post facto laws, judges tell you after the fact
whether or not they liked what you did. But there is no principle
involved—just "tension" that they can resolve any way they want to.

The very idea that there can be a principle is undermined when
Judge Sparks' opinion refers to "trying to reconcile the meaning of
words written over a century ago with the realities of the latter twentieth century." This is the now-familiar argument that changes in society have made necessary a change in the law.

Even if this argument is accepted, it is still a non sequitur to say
that judges are the ones to make the change. There are, after all,
elected officials who can decide whether a change is in order—and
what kind of change. They can also reconsider their decision if experience convinces them (or the voters) that they have made a mistake.

Words like "realities" and "tension" are blank checks for judges
to turn their prejudices into "the law of the land"—and to make their
mistakes uncorrectable. The particular mistakes that they make are
far less important than their undermining the very concept of the rule
of law. Arbitrary edicts from judges are not the rule of law, they are
the rule of lawlessness from the bench.

Judge Sparks repeats all the unsubstantiated cliches about affirmative action. For example, he seems convinced that he can tell "the
present effects of past discrimination," though he offers nothing concrete to support this dogma.

Why no such present effects of past discrimination seem dis-
cernible in the case of Asian Americans is a question neither asked
nor answered. Nor is there the slightest interest shown in whether
blacks in fact do better or worse in schools with a history of past ex-

clusion and discrimination. This whole line of reasoning—if it can be called that—is hermetically sealed off from any unpleasant confrontations with fact.

One of the most unpleasant facts of all is that minority students admitted with lower qualifications fail to graduate more often than students admitted under normal standards, whether these latter students are black or white. Those who do graduate tend to come in at the bottom of their class. Yet supposedly responsible adults seriously believe that this makes for better race relations.

Why did the University of Texas lose this case, if affirmative action is so right and so necessary? Because it had separate admissions procedures for white and minority applicants. Put them all in the same pool, giving minority students a "plus" factor and all will be well. It is the same distinction without a difference that earned such kudos for former Supreme Court Justice Lewis F. Powell in his *Bakke* decision back in 1978.

Another distinction without a difference by Judge Sparks is between a flexible "goal" and a rigid "quota." But the objection to a quota is that it is a quantitative rather than a qualitative criterion. It is body count rather than intellectual quality. Whether the quantitative criterion is flexible or rigid is incidental and a red herring.

Like so many unprincipled decisions, this one is rambling and verbose. Obviously, you cannot get to the point if there is no point to get to.

"CIVIL LIBERTIES"
PROTECTION

IT IS THE YEAR 2050.

"Hello. This is the headquarters of the American Civil Liberties Union. We are here to help safeguard your constitutional rights. Please listen carefully to the following choices and then press the appropriate button on your digital telephone. One of our attorneys will be with you shortly.

"If you are a welfare recipient who has been denied benefits, press one.

"If you have heard any references to religion in the public schools, press two.

"If you are a girl who has not been allowed to play on a boys' athletic team, press three."

"If you are a defendant in a criminal case and have had an unhappy childhood, press four.

"If you are a student who does not want to follow the dress code at your school, press five.

"If you have AIDS and don't think that the government has done enough for your benefit, press six."

"If you are a member of any racial, ethnic, or cultural minority whose demands have not been met, press seven."

Beep.

"Thank you for indicating that you are a member of a racial, ethnic, or cultural minority. We at the A.C.L.U. believe in diversity and are on your side. Our attorneys are here to fight injustices in our racist society. Please select from the following menu of choices.

"If you have been fired by a non-minority supervisor, press one.

"If you have been fired by a minority supervisor, press two.

"If your application for a bank loan was disapproved, press three.

"If you were given a traffic ticket by a policeman who seemed to be irritated with you, press four.

"If you overheard an ethnic joke, press five.

"If you were the first person your employer asked to play on the company's basketball team, press six.

"If you were the last person to be invited to join the company's chess team, press seven.

"All other injustices, press eight."

Beep.

"As a victim of miscellaneous injustices, you are entitled to the full protection of the law and to just compensation. Our attorneys will see that you get it. To help us to help you more effectively, please choose from the following menu.

"If you are over 65, press one.

"If you live on an Indian reservation, press two.

"If you are a woman, press three.

"If you served in the military, press four.

"If you refused to serve in the military, press five."

Beep.

"Thank you for indicating that you are a minority woman. That makes you doubly discriminated against. Our attorneys will be able to sue under twice as many laws for twice as much money. By all means stay on the line, and someone will be with you shortly. In the meantime, we will play some music of a non-religious nature, with no military beat, and selected with sensitivity to all minority cultural heritages."

(Music begins with "I am Woman.")

"Hello, welcome to the American Civil Liberties Union. My name is Forrest Sherwood and I will be your attorney. What is your name please?"

Silence.

"Will you please give me your name?"

"Oh, I'm sorry. I was waiting to hear when I was supposed to press the buttons."

"No, this is live now."

"Well, my name is Mary Wu."

"Ah, an Asian American! We don't get many of those. What injustice did you suffer?"

"Well, none actually."

"No injustice? In this racist society?"

"Nothing that I would consider an injustice."

"Are you sure you have the right number? This is the American Civil Liberties Union."

"I know. One of your employees dropped her purse in a parking lot and drove off before I could tell her. So I am calling to find out how I can return it."

THE MEANING OF LAW

ELLIE NESLER IS THE MOTHER of a sexually abused child who shot dead the man who was in court to face charges of being the guilty party.

Strong feelings have been aroused on both sides of this issue. There are people collecting money to defend Nessler and others who are denouncing the "vigilante" actions of people who take the law into their own hands.

We all understand why people should not take the law into their own hands. A civilized society would not be possible if everyone did that. Unfortunately, many of those who condemn this woman have been strangely silent for more than 30 years as all sorts of other people have taken the law into their own hands for all sorts of other reasons.

For no one should taking the law into their own hands be more inexcusable than for judges, who not only know better but who have sworn to uphold the law. Yet judges at all levels, up to and including the Supreme Court, have been applauded for deciding cases on the basis of fashionable social theories, rather than the written law.

Indeed, one of the reasons for the bitter frustration of people like Ellie Nesler is that courts have become a plaything of the anointed, rather than an instrument for upholding the laws of the land. The man she killed had already been convicted of sexual molestation before and had been let off with wrist-slap "punishment."

Judges have made it increasingly difficult for American society to protect itself from anyone or anything, by creating new "rights" out of thin air and by leaning over backward for the benefit of those with anti-social behavior.

In short, judges have taken the law into their own hands, instead of carrying out the laws duly passed by democratically elected representatives, reflecting the concerns of a self-governing people. The pretense that judges do this to uphold the constitution is wearing so thin that growing numbers of people now see this as the fraud that it is.

For more than a century and a half after the constitution was written, the greatest legal minds in the history of the Supreme Court failed to discover these new criminal "rights" discovered by intellectual lightweights and ideological zealots on the High Court during the past 30 years.

Such judges have taken the law into their own hands—and that is ultimately why Ms. Nesler took the law into her own hands, to defend her child when the law refuses to defend him. Many of those who condemn her are all too willing to let judges play fast and loose with the law, provided they end up with "politically correct" decisions.

When people ask for Supreme Court justices with "compassion" or with "sensitivity," what are they asking for, except people who will lean the way they want justices to lean?

An even-handed application of rules is a demanding job and a heavy responsibility. Even an umpire cannot have "compassion" or "sensitivity." He can either call them honestly as he sees them or prostitute his profession by leaning toward pitchers or batters or base runners.

When courts of law become courts of political correctness, those who suffer are not just those who lose particular cases. The whole society loses. Law exists for a reason—and that reason is not so that judges can indulge their own egos or flatter themselves that their squeamishness is a higher morality.

American society today is polarized over the issue of abortion, not simply because people have different opinions on the subject—which they always have—but because Justice Harry Blackmun imposed his own social opinion under the dishonest pretense of discovering a constitutional "right" that no one else had ever found in the constitution.

He took the law into his own hands—and was roundly applauded by many of the same people who now condemn the anguished mother of a traumatized child.

This same spirit of playing fast and loose with the law, in order to impose a social agenda or "make a statement" has spread downward from the Supreme Court to other appellate courts and into the trial courts.

Nothing has been more deeply embedded, for centuries, in the Anglo-American legal traditions than the notion that the accused is innocent until proven guilty. Yet there are both civil rights and antitrust cases where only a few flimsy statistics are enough to force the accused to try to prove his innocence.

This perversion of the law is not only accepted but applauded because it reaches politically correct conclusions. Radical feminists are in fact working hard to extend this presumption of guilt to those accused of sexual harassment.

If we are going to condemn people who take the law into their own hands, let us start with those who are sworn to uphold the law, who cold-bloodedly decide to twist that law to their own purposes, not with an overwrought mother whose child has been victimized because the law was lax.

POWER TO THE PARASITES

IT MAY BE A LANDMARK IN THE HISTORY of American business—and of American society—if Dow Corning's filing for bankruptcy is the beginning of the end for this corporation. Lawsuits for huge damages against the company for its silicon breast implants are behind this latest development.

It is not that these implants have been proven to cause medical problems. Rather, it has been unnecessary to prove anything in order to get cases put before juries who are free to hand out other people's money in whatever amounts strike their fancy, in response to whatever appeals the plaintiff's lawyers make.

Scientific study after scientific study has failed to turn up evidence to substantiate the claims made by those suing Dow Corning over breast implants. Meanwhile, back in the courts, judges and juries are handing out multimillion dollar awards in damages.

The fate of one corporation is not a major national issue but what it implies about our whole system of justice has grim implications for the future of this country. As a critic said, more than half a century ago, "Law has lost its soul and become jungle." That is even more true today.

The media have a heavy responsibility in all this. Their willingness to serve as a megaphone for all sorts of politically correct groups and movements has sent them off and running like a pack of hounds after any business accused of anything by the radical feminists, the environmentalists, or other favorites of the anointed.

The very idea that the burden of proof is on the party who makes a legal charge has gone out the window as far as whole categories of charges are concerned. This is nowhere more true than in so-called "women's issues" but it is also true in racial issues, environmental issues and other crusades pushed by strident activists.

More than individual injustices are involved. A whole class of parasites has been created and sanctified, ranging from the panhandlers in the streets to the lawyers in the suites. You can believe that Dow Corning will not be the last of their prey.

All over this country, doctors, local governments, corporations, universities, and many others are being targeted for lawsuits by attorneys on the prowl wherever there is money to be had. Anyone with a "deep pocket" is fair game. And many of these deep pockets are nothing more than a lot of much shallower pockets of taxpayers and stockholders.

Two centuries ago, British statesman Edmund Burke warned of the dangers to any society that promotes the idea that some of its citizens are the natural prey of others. Yet that is not only what the litigation explosion is all about. It is what all the political talk of "the rich" is all about.

This is the age of the complaining classes, whether they are lawyers, community activists, radical feminists, race hustlers, or other squeaking wheels looking for oil.

No society ever thrived because it had a large and growing class of parasites living off those who produce. On the contrary, the growth of a large parasitic class marked the decline and fall of the Roman Empire and the collapse of Spain from the heights of its golden age.

Despite Karl Marx's use of the term "proletariat" to describe the working class, the Roman proletariat was not so much a working class as an underclass supported by government handouts. But the parasites in ancient Rome also included a large and growing bureaucracy. The Byzantine Empire and later the Ottoman Empire likewise developed over the centuries bureaucracies so suffocating and corrupt as to bring their eras of glory to an end.

More than a thousand years after the collapse of Rome, Spain used the wealth it extracted from its vast empire to support growing numbers of Spaniards in idleness. Not only were vagabonds begging everywhere, there were also large numbers of educated parasites with no skills to use to add to the country's output but with big ideas about how that its wealth ought to be spent.

No small part of our social problems today come from miseducated degree-holders who have nothing to contribute to the wealth of the society but who are full of demands and indignation—and resentment of those who are producing.

A study of the decline of great societies concluded that "disappearances of empires due to catastrophes have been extremely rare in history." Rather, they slowly but steadily corrode and crumble from within. There is usually "a growing amount of wealth pumped by the State from the economy," while "extravagances of fashion and license" develop among the people. Does this sound uncomfortably similar to what we see around us today?

CRIMINALS AND COURTS

OFTEN, IN SPORTS, THE WINNER was no more skilled or talented than the loser but simply "wanted it more," as they say. That may be why crime has grown so dramatically over the past 30 years. The criminals are more serious about what they are doing. They are more determined to win.

The police may also be determined to win, but the courts have the last word on what the police can do—and they have the last word on what is done to the criminals after they are caught and convicted. According to statistics from the Pacific Legal Foundation, violent crime is today 5 times as prevalent as it was back in 1960.

Some of the reasons may be found in how criminals are treated. Three out of four convicted criminals are not incarcerated at all. Nationwide, criminals serve less than 37 percent of their sentences. Why then are they given sentences in court that do not mean what they say?

Those sentences are not meant to determine how long criminals stay behind bars. They are meant to mollify people like you and me by letting us think that some serious sentences are being handed out for serious crimes.

Many of the people who write the laws, who sit as judges or who serve on parole boards are convinced that they know so much better than the rest of us poor dumb slobs how to handle criminals. Phony sentences keep the public happy, while reduced sentences and "rehabilitation" through psycho-babble are supposed to deal with the crime problem.

The net result is that even murderers are in jail less than 8 years. And of course they may be on the street periodically on "furlough" even during those years—and of course commit other crimes, including murder, while taking part in these wonderful programs dreamed up by the anointed.

A study of more than 100,000 former prisoners showed that 63 percent of them were rearrested for serious crimes, including more than 2,000 murders. Even the phrase "life in prison without the possibility of parole" means less than meets the eye. A multiple murderer in Puerto Rico with such a sentence was released last fall by the retiring governor. Other murderers under similar sentences have escaped, killed while on furlough, or killed in prison.

Criminals understand that they are at war with society. But many of those whose jobs it is to protect society do not want to treat criminals like mortal enemies. Too many judges and members of parole boards devote their authority to massaging their own egos instead of protecting society.

Some years ago, when a young, black teenage girl I know was raped by a hoodlum released by some judge, I thought: Somewhere out there in the affluent suburbs, there is a white liberal judge who feels good about himself because he gave a ghetto youth another chance.

Many of those who began the current legal trends back in the 1960s began with a vision in which the problems of the world—crime included—exist only because ordinary people do not have all the wonderful special insights and deep moral commitments that the anointed like themselves have. Their first order of business, therefore, is to brush aside what ordinary people think, mollify them with rhetoric and phoney sentences if need be, but instead engage in social experiments designed to get at the "root causes" of crime, rehabilitate criminals and perform miscellaneous other miracles as needed.

Have three decades of disastrous experience with this approach—and the soaring crime rates that followed—taught them nothing? Well, not much.

While the political left today may not have the boundless confidence with which people like Chief Justice Earl Warren or Attorney General Ramsey Clark proclaimed the new approach to crime back in the 1960s, nevertheless it could be devastating to their egos to admit that their moral preening had unleashed the runaway crime that has blighted many lives and snuffed out many others.

The anointed are going to believe any other explanation, however strained, before they believe that. Far better to believe that crime is caused by the "neglect" of "society" than to believe that you have blood on your own hands. Far better to keep on trying a failed approach than to look at yourself in the mirror and realize what monstrous crimes have resulted from your own petty vanity.

There is always a war going on between criminals and the rest of society. Over the past generation, however, too many people in "responsible" positions have forgotten that, while taking an ego trip instead of fighting back.

THE WAR AGAINST
CLARENCE THOMAS

THERE SEEM TO BE TWO CLARENCE THOMASES, who are no relation
to each other. There is Supreme Court Justice Clarence Thomas,
whom I read about in the liberal media, and then there is the man of
the same name whom I have known for more than a dozen years. You
could hardly find two people who are more different.

In order to explain away Justice Thomas' decisive votes in two
recent Supreme Court decisions, law professor [Herman] Schwartz
said: "He must be a deeply embittered man."

Not to worry, Herman. Clarence Thomas is one of the most
cheerful people I know. Just last week, I was feeling a little down and
phoned him to get a more upbeat view of things. Sure enough, he was
in high spirits and soon had me laughing.

Professor Schwartz, however, is not just another amateur shrink.
He is all too typical of the self-righteous intelligentsia, who cannot
imagine how anyone could possibly disagree with them, without being mentally incompetent, morally flawed or psychologically
twisted—preferably all three.

The fact that Clarence Thomas was angry at the way he had been
treated by the Senate Judiciary Committee back in 1991 has been
seized upon by media pundits to claim that his decisions on the
Supreme Court reflect that bitterness. Yet those who practice this
kind of pop psychology never bother to show how his decisions since
then differ in any way whatever from the kinds of decisions he made
on the Circuit Court of Appeals—or the kind of philosophy he expressed years before he ever sat on any court.

It so happens that I talked with Clarence Thomas the morning after he gave the Senate Judiciary Committee a piece of his mind on
nationwide television. He sounded more upbeat than he had sounded

146

in months. He showed not the slightest concern as to whether or not the Senators would confirm his appointment to the Supreme Court. He had gotten things off his chest and was like a new man.

People who win are not embittered. People who lose are embittered. It is the liberals who lost big in their attempt to destroy this man by the same character assassination tactics that had worked in derailing the nomination of Judge Robert Bork four years earlier. That Justice Thomas continues to have the same judicial philosophy that caused them to oppose him in the first place may embitter them, but there is no point projecting that onto him.

As far as the charges made by Anita Hill, there is not the slightest reason for him to dwell on them. Think about it: Clarence Thomas is one of only two people in this country who has never had to spend a single moment trying to figure out who was telling the truth.

Some people were astonished at the time that he took a nap while Anita Hill was testifying. But what could she tell him? He was there. When something didn't happen, why would you be interested in the details of what didn't happen?

The true lasting bitterness has been that of Justice Thomas' critics who lost. As I came out of the White House grounds after watching the ceremony in which he was presented by President Bush after being confirmed, I saw a young blond woman carrying a picket sign saying: "He's still not qualified!"

Even Yogi Berra would have said that it was all over at that point. But the political left cannot let it be.

Whenever I hear someone take a cheap shot at Clarence Thomas' qualifications, I ask them: "Have you ever read a single opinion of his?" There hasn't been a "yes" yet.

It so happens that I have read many of his judicial opinions, going all the way back to when he was on the Circuit Court of Appeals. I have also read the judicial opinions of Thurgood Marshall, with whom Justice Thomas is often compared unfavorably. I defy anybody who knows what logic is, and who can separate legal reasoning from policy preferences, to show me anything that Thurgood Marshall ever wrote that can come close to the quality of the judicial analysis of Clarence Thomas.

Last year, the head of a well-known east coast think tank, who was educated at one of the leading law schools, said that Justice Thomas' opinion in *Holder v. hall* was the best example of legal reasoning in the Supreme Court all that year. More recently, when Margaret Carlin of *Time* magazine took a cheap shot at Clarence Thomas on the "Capital Gang" program, panelist Bob Novak shot back that the justice's legal analysis was "brilliant."

The next day, when I played back my telephone answering machine, I found a message from an attorney with a prominent law firm. He left a whole string of superlatives praising Justice Thomas' performance. This attorney had called me on something completely unrelated.

History will of course render the final verdict on Clarence Thomas. But he is young enough to find vindication—and more— within his own lifetime.

A SETBACK FOR LYNCH LAW

AMID MUCH LARGER EVENTS, THE RELEASE of John Demjanjuk by the Israeli Supreme Court seems to have attracted relatively little notice. Yet its implications go deeper than one man's case and apply far beyond the borders of Israel.

When the Israeli Supreme Court overturned the conviction of John Demjanjuk, who was accused of being the sadistic Nazi concentration camp guard "Ivan the Terrible," it not only made a legal decision, it made a statement about law, about Israel, and about honor and courage.

They set an example we could all imitate.

What this decision means, most of all, is that—no matter how heinous the crime—guilt must still be proved. This basic foundation of law has been continuously undermined in the United States in recent years, by those who think that some accusations, such as child abuse or sexual harassment, are to be believed automatically.

That's not law. That's lynch law, even if it happens in a courtroom.

People have spent years behind bars on child abuse charges that appellate courts later found to be unbelievably flimsy. Zealots want convictions, and they are not always careful about how they get them. Some activists openly say that when a child doesn't remember any abuse, that only shows how traumatic it was.

The lynch law spirit has also been directed at people like columnist Pat Buchanan, who publicly questioned the deportation and conviction of Demjanjuk long ago. The lynch law spirit may also have been at work in the Justice Department, which threw away evidence that might have cast doubt on the case against Demjanjuk.

The issue is not whether Demjanjuk is innocent, as the Israeli Supreme Court well understood. Law is infinitely more important than Demjanjuk. Whether or not he was guilty of other things in other places, the Court did not find the evidence sufficiently compelling to convict him of what he was charged with.

When judges in a nation whose people have suffered the horrors of the Holocaust can still uphold the law, what excuse can there be for the wishy-washy decisions of the U. S. Supreme Court, trying to split the difference and be all things to all people?

What excuse can there be for spineless college administrators on elite college campuses across the country, where it is an open secret that academic rules and rules of conduct are applied or not applied according to whether or not those involved belong to a group that is or is not "politically correct." The next generation of Americans is being "educated" in lawlessness and lynch law.

Respect for law does not mean mushiness toward criminals. It has been suggested, for example, that Demjanjuk should be re-admitted to the United States, since he was deprived of his citizenship as a result of Justice Department misconduct. But if Demjanjuk gained admission to this country by lying about his past, that is sufficient reason to keep him from returning here.

The notion that misconduct in law enforcement should be dealt with by letting law violators get away with their own misconduct has cost this country dearly. It has cost some people their lives, as vicious criminals have been turned loose on ever more strained technicalities to prey on the public again.

Criminal justice is not some kind of sporting contest. It is part of a war between those who threaten society and those who are trying to preserve it and protect the people in it.

If someone in the Justice Department was guilty of misconduct, then that should be dealt with separately—not turned into a windfall gain for Demjanjuk. There is too much of that kind of fuzzy thinking already.

We need only look at Los Angeles, where a felon who recklessly endangered human lives and resisted arrest is now not only getting off Scot free, but is likely to become a millionaire at the taxpayers' expense—not to mention a folk hero in some quarters—because of what the police did to him.

In the case of Demjanjuk, the Israeli Supreme Court simply said that it was freeing him "because of doubt." This was not a finding of innocence and no vindication. Just a carrying out of the law.

Eyewitness identifications of Demjanjuk after more than forty years have to raise doubts, no matter how sincerely convinced the witnesses may have been that he was their tormentor. I can recall from my own school days a boy named Henry who looked so much like me that another boy who was angry at me jumped on Henry by mistake.

It was quite a mistake because Henry was the toughest kid in the class.

In our world of soft options, expediency and just plain cop-outs, can you imagine what it must have been like for judges in Israel to free a man accused of being a concentration camp guard for the Nazis? Can you imagine what it must have been like to be an Israeli lawyer defending him?

Their courage and integrity were not only a proud achievement for Israel. It was a proud moment for the concept of law—and for everything that depends upon law.

MASCOTS OF THE ANOINTED

THE *NEW YORK TIMES* RECENTLY RAN a front page story dripping with sympathy for a multiple murderer who is now very old and who, on some days, "cannot remember" why he is in prison. His victims, however, cannot remember anything on any days.

There are also photographs of him and other prisoners. One prisoner is described as having a disease that "brings mental deterioration." Another, with his legs amputated, is shown trying to catch a baseball on his knees. Yet another prisoner is shown in a wheelchair.

All sorts of heart-tugging stories are told about elderly inmates who are succumbing to various diseases and infirmities of age. There are, however, no stories at all about their victims, or their victims' widows or orphans, or how tough their lives have been.

Although the *Times* runs this as a "news" story, it is in effect a long editorial on how terrible it is to keep these prisoners locked up, years after they have ceased to be dangerous to society. This one-sided presentation includes the views of the American Civil Liberties Union and prison officials who would like to use the space taken up by these elderly prisoners. But there is not one word from a victim or from police who have had to deal with these killers.

Bias shades off into propaganda when the *Times* quotes ACLU figures that there are more than 30,000 prisoners who are 50 or older in the nation's prisons. Note that we started out with stories about people so old and infirm that they are supposedly no danger to anyone. Now we get statistics that are not about such people at all but about people "50 or older."

I don't know what would make the *New York Times* or the American Snivel Liberties Union suggest that people cease to be dangerous at 50. I am older than that and I fired a rifle and a shotgun just a few days ago. We old codgers can still pull a trigger.

One of the murderers featured in the *Times'* own story was 74 years old when he began serving his life sentence. What a shame he did not realize how harmless he was after age 50.

The propaganda game of talking about one thing and citing statistics about something else has been used in many other contexts. Stories about violence against women often begin with terrible individual tragedies and then move on to numbers about "abuse," which include such things as a husband's stomping out of the room after an argument. Statistics about serious violence against women are less than one-tenth as large as the numbers that are thrown around in the media by feminist activists. Moreover, serious violence against men is about twice as high.

In technique, as well as in bias, the *Times* story about criminals is classic liberal propaganda for one of their mascot groups. But this is not something peculiar to the *New York Times.* You can find the same kinds of stories in the *Washington Post* or the *Los Angeles Times,* or on any of the leading television networks.

Criminals are just one of the groups adopted as mascots of the media. All sorts of parasites and predators have been displayed as if they were ocelots or other exotic creatures that adorn the world of the anointed. The deeper question is: Why is it necessary for the anointed to have human mascots? And why do they choose the kind of people that they do?

Whoever is condemned by society at large—criminals, vagrants, illegal aliens, AIDS-carriers, etc.—are eligible to become mascots of the anointed, symbols of their superior wisdom and virtue. By lavishing concern on those we condemn, the anointed become morally one-up on the rest of us.

Is that important? To some it is paramount. A quarter of a century before the Gettysburg Address, Abraham Lincoln said in a speech in Springfield, Illinois, that the greatest danger to the future of the United States would come, not from foreign enemies, but from that class of people which "thirsts and burns for distinction."

These people could not find that distinction "in supporting and maintaining an edifice that has been erected by others," according to

Lincoln. In other words, there is not nearly as much ego satisfaction in building up this country as in tearing it down.

For example, a Stanford law student involved in the "prisoner's rights" movement said recently, "it's precisely because prisoners are viewed as the castaways of our society—that's what draws me to them even more." She wants to know "why a person can't function in this society, what it is about this society."

Our schools and colleges are today turning out more and more people like this, who are taught to despise American society and to boost their own egos by blaming that society for sins that are common among human beings around the world. Journalism is just one of the professions being prostituted to this self-indulgence.

THE DEATH PENALTY

NOW THAT NEW YORK'S NEW GOVERNOR, George Pataki, has come out in favor of the death penalty that Mario Cuomo opposed for so many years, the defenders of murderers have sprung into action. A feature story in the *New York Times* was headed: "The Rage to Kill Those Who Kill."

The title was a gem. It explained away others' beliefs as mere emotion—"rage"—and created a false moral equivalence. According to the deep thinkers, executing murderers is "repeating the acts that society condemns." Physical equivalence becomes moral equivalence.

If we took this kind of "reasoning" seriously, it would be wrong to take back by force what a robber has seized by force. It would be wrong to imprison someone who had illegally imprisoned someone else. It would be wrong for the police to drive above the speed limit to pursue someone who was speeding.

No ordinary person with common sense confuses physical equivalence with moral equivalence. Only deep thinkers on a crusade do that.

The grand dogma of the opponents of the death penalty is that executions do not deter murder. A 1959 study on which this dogma was based was so crude that it was laughable. But it told the anointed what they wanted to hear.

A more sophisticated study, by Professor Isaac Ehrlich of the University of Chicago, indicated that eight murders were deterred by every execution. The anointed jumped all over him, making all sorts of objections to his statistical methods that they never made against the study that supported their prejudices.

One of the problems with statistical studies on this subject is that the era when executions were common and murder rates were low was also an era of sloppy statistics, with all sorts of "homicides"— including fatal automobile accidents—sometimes being included.

Since the death penalty has applied to premeditated murder, it was never intended to deter automobile accidents. And now that the statistics are better kept, executions are so rare and so long delayed that high statistical correlations are not to be expected.

But we do not require high statistical correlations for most policies on most issues. Moreover, we know that the death penalty definitely deters those who are executed. The fact that this is obvious does not make it any less important.

It is certainly not less important to the families of people murdered by those who have murdered before and who have been turned loose by judges or parole boards, or allowed weekend furloughs by "progressive" prison authorities. Whether these additional murders meet the statisticians' technical definitions of "significance," they are very significant to widows, orphans and the parents of murdered children.

"Life in prison without the possibility of parole" is the grand alternative to execution presented by those who consider words equivalent to reality. But there is nothing to prevent people under such a sentence from being paroled under later laws or later court rulings. Moreover, there is nothing to stop them from escaping or from killing again while in prison.

One of the most dishonest arguments against the death penalty is that it costs more to execute someone than to keep them alive. That may well be true in itself, but it is precisely the kind of people who oppose the death penalty who have promoted all kinds of delaying tactics and judicial rulings that make it possible for even the most clear-cut murder conviction to take more than a decade to end with an execution.

The Supreme Court got us into this legal mess by pretending to find a prohibition or restriction against capital punishment implicit in the Constitution, rather than in the fashionable writings of the anointed. While the 8th Amendment forbids "cruel and unusual punishment," the 5th Amendment—passed at the same time—accepted the legality of the death penalty by saying that it must take place through "due process of law."

This twisting and straining of the law by judges reflects the same influences as the twisting and straining of logic by others among the anointed who confuse squeamishness with higher morality. More fundamentally, however, the death penalty is another in a long series of issues which provide occasions for moral preening and presumptions of deeper wisdom which lie at the heart of the vision of the anointed—whether the issue is crime, foreign policy, or health care.

Most of those who oppose capital punishment tend to oppose punishment in general and to favor "rehabilitation," getting at the "root causes" of crime and other notions that have failed disastrously and repeatedly.

One of the reasons so many liberal schemes have continued to be defended, long after they have turned out to be counterproductive, is that conceding that a particular policy has been mistaken is not merely a policy issue. Such a damaging admission can bring a whole vision of oneself crashing down in ruins.

Naturally, the anointed resist that bitterly. Unfortunately, others pay the price of this bitter-end resistance to reality.

PART V
THE RACIAL SCENE

MISTAKEN IDENTITY

When a couple of black kids were being boisterous in a public place, their aunt let them know that she was unhappy and embarrassed by their misbehaving. One of the kids said: "Why do white people get to make the rules about how we behave?'

No white people had been mentioned, but already these children had picked up the message that how they talked and acted was their own business and that any constraints put on them was white people's doing—and a violation of their black "identity."

The tragedy and the farce in all this is that what these children—and many older people—see as black identity is in fact a cultural legacy left over from ignorant whites in times past.

What the multiculturalists call "black English" is a dialect that existed in parts of southern and western England three centuries ago. As often happens, this cultural legacy survived where it was transplanted—to the American South—longer than it survived where it originated. And it survived longer among blacks in the urban ghettos than it survived among Southern whites.

The same has been true of a whole spectrum of things—from something as incidental as playing the card game whist to a boisterous, wisecracking, violent lifestyle. The term "crackers," for example, originated in Britain to describe the wisecracking ancestors of people who later moved to the Southern United States.

Illegitimacy, illiteracy, and a whole set of attitudes toward work and toward life were part of a distinctive culture that travelled across the ocean from Britain to the American South, just as a very different way of life crossed the ocean with people from other parts of Britain who went to New England and other regions.

Those ghetto youths who think that talking jive, playing whist, getting girls pregnant and being belligerent are all part of black identity do not realize how much they are just being crackers with darker complexions.

In the past, over a period of generations, education and rising economic and social standards eroded this kind of self-destructive culture, among both whites and blacks. The more fortunate and more educated people of both races were the first to discard this way of life. But those who were poorer and less educated tended to discard this counterproductive lifestyle later.

By the 1960s, millions of blacks had escaped this essentially redneck culture—as millions of whites had. But now the new cult of "identity," romanticized—or at least "understood"—this lifestyle among ghetto blacks and treated any criticism of it as racism.

Exempting any group of people from criticism is not a blessing but a curse. One of the reasons so many kings did so many self-destructive things in centuries past—things which sometimes cost them their kingdoms or even their heads—was that they were surrounded by people who flattered them, instead of telling them the truth.

Young people in the ghettos do not have any kingdoms to lose. They only have a future to lose. That future is going to belong to whoever can function in the increasingly high-tech, internationally competitive world. Those who cling to the obsolete past are going to be left behind.

In the normal course of events, cultural characteristics come and go, as people decide what to treasure and what to discard. That is why most blacks and most whites no longer behave as they did before a changing world led them to adjust to new circumstances and new opportunities. But those blacks who have not yet made it beyond the cultural handicaps of the past are being encouraged to cling to this millstone around their necks.

Why? Because such blacks have been adopted as mascots by the white counterculture. There has even been a federal case over teachers' attempts to get ghetto students to speak standard English rather than "black English."

It is great fun for countercultural whites to tweak the establishment by championing the cause of anti-social behavior among blacks. It also helps them to feel morally one-up on those who criticize such behavior. Blacks are the mascots of these whites.

What all this does for blacks is a different story. Mascots serve a symbolic purpose for others but what actually happens to the mascots themselves is usually of little concern.

It would be sad enough if people painted themselves into a corner by clinging to an authentic culture that was now obsolete. To do so for a culture that represents somebody else's leftovers is truly tragic.

DOG-IN-THE-MANGER POLITICS

A PLASTIC SURGEON OF CHINESE ancestry in Sydney, Australia, may not sound like an average individual, but the moral of his story is all too common in countries around the world. Born in Malaysia, this plastic surgeon was in one of many high-level positions occupied by the Chinese minority and coveted by the Malay majority. Moreover, under the country's affirmative action policies, he understood that his days as a plastic surgeon were numbered.

He took it all without bitterness, offering to stay on to treat disfigured children and others until a Malay plastic surgeon was available to replace him. But he missed the point. They wanted him out of there, whether or not there was a Malay to replace him and whether or not disfigured people had anyone else to turn to.

The surgeon relocated to Australia, where he was apparently doing quite well by the time I encountered him. The real victims of the Malaysian government's policies were still in Malaysia.

This dog-in-the-manger approach is by no means peculiar to Malaysia. Envy of others' success and embarrassment at being visibly unable to match their performance have been political driving forces behind many programs of preferences and quotas.

When Romania acquired additional territory from the defeated Central Powers after the First World War, it also acquired universities which were culturally either German or Hungarian.

One of their top priorities was to get rid of the Germans and the Hungarians on the faculties and transform the universities into Romanian bastions.

At that point, roughly three-quarters of all Romanians were still illiterate, so replacing these foreign professors with Romanians of comparable caliber was very unlikely. But replacement was not the issue: Getting rid of those who were better qualified was the issue.

Despite all the zeal expended in converting German and Hungarian universities in the new provinces of Bukovina and Transylvania into Romanian universities, there was no urgency at all about creating a university in the province of Bessarabia, where none existed. Moreover, when Hungarian students living in Romania began going to Hungary to attend universities there, the Romanian government forbad them to do so.

What is involved is not just envy. It is the threat to one's ego that is crucial in promoting dog-in-the-manger policies. When Nigeria became an independent nation, back in the 1960s, many of the educated, skilled, business and professional people in northern Nigeria were from tribes in southern Nigeria.

One of the top priorities of northern Nigerian politicians was to get rid of such people. The hope was to replace them eventually with northern Nigerians. But, in the meantime, the northern Nigerians wanted them out of there, even if they had to hire Europeans to replace them or suffer a deterioration of the services being performed by the southern Nigerians.

Having Europeans in these occupations was far less of a threat to the ego than having fellow Africans so dramatically outperforming the locals.

Such attitudes are not unknown in the United States, whether or not ethnic or racial differences are involved. The same dog-in-the-manger can be found when the issue is class. Liberals have never ceased denouncing Ronald Reagan's "tax cuts for the rich" in the early 1980s, despite the actual results, including a record-breaking period of economic expansion.

After the tax *rate* was cut on the highest income brackets (and on others), not only did the total tax *receipts* rise but the percentage of those receipts paid by "the rich" also rose. Why then were the liberals unhappy? Because those in the upper brackets paid these vastly greater taxes out of rising incomes, while retaining a higher percentage of those incomes for themselves.

The dog-in-the-manger principle requires that the rich be made worse off. Any policy that fails to do that has failed politically, regardless of what economic benefits it may bring to the society as a whole.

While such attitudes are sufficiently widespread around the world that they cannot be attributed to a particular culture, neither are they inevitable. Very often, the key ingredient in the rise of explosive resentments is the rise of an intelligentsia preoccupied with invidious comparisons rather than general well-being.

Ironically, all too often the rich themselves have been the patrons of such intellectuals, whether at the universities, the foundations or other institutions supported by their donations.

THE SLAVERY CARD

ONE OF THE MANY SAD SIGNS of our times is that people are not only playing the race card, they are playing the slavery card, which is supposedly the biggest trump of all. At the so-called "million man march" in Washington, poet Maya Angelou rang all the changes on slavery, at a rally billed as forward-looking and as being about black independence rather than white guilt. Meanwhile, best-selling author Dinesh D'Souza was being denounced in the media for having said that slavery was not a racist institution.

First of all, anyone familiar with the history of slavery around the world knows that its origins go back thousands of years and that slaves and slaveowners were very often of the same race. Those who are ignorant of all this, or who think of slavery in the United States as if it were the only slavery, go ballistic when anyone tells them that this institution was not based on race.

Blacks were not enslaved because they were black, but because they were available at the time. Whites enslaved other whites in Europe for centuries before the first black slave was brought to the Western Hemisphere.

Only late in history were human beings even capable of crossing an ocean to get millions of other human beings of a different race. In the thousands of years before that, not only did Europeans enslave other Europeans, Asians enslaved other Asians, Africans enslaved other Africans, and the native peoples of the Western Hemisphere enslaved other native peoples of the Western Hemisphere.

D'Souza was right. Slavery was not about race. The fact that his critics are ignorant of history is their problem.

What was peculiar about the American situation was not just that slaves and slaveowners were of different races, but that slavery contradicted the whole philosophy of freedom on which the society was founded. If all men were created equal, as the Declaration of Independence said, then blacks had to be depicted as less than men.

While the antebellum South produced a huge volume of apologetic literature trying to justify slavery on racist grounds, no such justification was considered necessary in vast reaches of the world and over vast expanses of time. In most parts of the world, people saw nothing wrong with slavery.

Strange as that seems to us today, a hundred years ago only Western civilization saw anything wrong with slavery. And two hundred years ago, only a minority in the West thought it was wrong.

Africans, Arabs, Asians and others not only maintained slavery long after it was abolished throughout the Western Hemisphere, they resisted all attempts of the West to stamp out slavery in their lands during the age of imperialism. Only the fact that the West had greater firepower and more economic and political clout enabled them to impose the abolition of slavery, as they imposed other Western ideas, on the non-Western world.

Those who talk about slavery as if it were just the enslavement of blacks by whites ignore not only how widespread this institution was and how far back in history it went, they also ignore how recently slavery continued to exist outside of Western civilization.

While slavery was destroyed in the West during the nineteenth century, the struggle to end slavery elsewhere continued well into the twentieth century. In Mauritania it was officially abolished just 15 years ago, though even its own officials admitted that it still continued, as it does to this day.

There are 30,000 Africans enslaved in Mauritania under terrible conditions at this moment, but there is scarcely a peep about it from black "leaders" in America who thunder about slavery in the past.

If slavery were the real issue, then slavery among flesh-and-blood human beings alive today would arouse far more outcry than past slavery among people who are long dead. The difference is that past slavery can be cashed in for political benefits today, while slavery in North Africa only distracts from these political goals. Worse yet, talking about slavery in Africa would undermine the whole picture of unique white guilt requiring unending reparations.

While the Western world was just as guilty as other civilizations when it came to enslaving people for thousands of years, it was unique only in finally deciding that the whole institution was immoral and should be ended. But this conclusion was by no means universal even in the Western world, however obvious it may seem to us today.

Thousands of free blacks owned slaves in the antebellum South. And, years after the Emancipation Proclamation in the United States, whites as well as blacks were still being bought and sold as slaves in North Africa and the Middle East.

Anyone who wants reparations based on history will have to gerrymander history very carefully. Otherwise, practically everybody would owe reparations to practically everybody else.

ONE MAN'S EDUCATION

OF ALL THE THINGS I HAVE WRITTEN, what gave me the most immediate personal satisfaction were a couple of little-noticed and long-forgotten articles in the early 1970s on black schools with high academic standards. Since everyone seemed to be writing about the academic problems of black students, I thought someone should try to find out which educational approaches had actually worked with such students.

It was quite an emotional experience to see ghetto youngsters, many from families on welfare, performing at a high academic level, speaking in complete sentences with correct English and reasoning with logic and insight. Nor were these just some hand-picked individuals being shown off to me. In one particularly outstanding school in a Brooklyn ghetto, I walked down the halls with the principal and arbitrarily picked which classrooms I wanted to go into. Moreover, I did this on every floor in the building.

The test scores backed up what I had seen with my own eyes. This school's scores were far above those of similar schools in the same district and were comparable to what was found in much higher-income neighborhoods.

At the end of the day, when I waved goodbye to the kids in the school yard, I was on the verge of tears. Why couldn't this be done in other ghetto schools across the country? At the very least, I hoped that my report on all this would provide some clues to those trying to improve education for minority students.

Nothing could have been further from the reality. Not only were my articles widely ignored, where they did attract any attention from educators or civil rights activists, the first order of business seemed to be to try to discredit what I found. The children I studied were declared to be "middle class" and their experience therefore inapplicable to other black youngsters.

No one who dismissed these students as "middle class" offered a speck of evidence that they were. When I thought back to the run-down neighborhoods in which some of these schools were located, the ancient and battered buildings in which such high achievements took place, the comments of the critics seemed like something out of Alice in Wonderland.

This was one of the first of many painful lessons about educational issues and racial issues. To me the issue was simply how we might get better education for kids who needed it. But others in politics, in the civil rights movement, and in the educational establishment had completely different agendas. My articles were absolutely useless for those agendas.

What I found and wrote about would not justify any new government spending, any political crusades, or the aggrandizement of any racial "leaders." Neither money nor power could be gotten from what I said. Fundamentally, no one really cared whether it was true. It was a nuisance to be gotten rid of.

Another early and painful lesson I learned, in the late 1960s, came from working as a consultant to the Urban Coalition, developing a plan to provide scholarships and loans to enable low-income students to go to college. After months of work, travel, and conferring with people in academic, business and civic organizations, I drafted a plan which would have put money directly into the hands of the students. There was nothing in it for any educational institution, social movement, or politicians.

Although I was able to get business executives from Lytton Industries and A.T.& T. to fly to Washington for a conference on this plan at the Urban Coalition headquarters, the head of the Washington chapter of the N.A.A.C.P. wouldn't even walk down the street to attend the meeting. It didn't advance their agenda, even though it could advance the people for whom they claimed to speak.

In later years, as I began to get into more controversial issues, I discovered similar attitudes and agendas. When discussing affirmative action, the first question I would ask those who favored it was: "What hard evidence do you have that this has actually made minority working people better off, on net balance?"

Many seemed to think that this was some kind of trick question. But my research, first in the United States and then in other countries with similar programs, led me to conclude that affirmative action helps primarily those who are already more fortunate. Poorer members of the groups supposedly being helped have actually fallen further behind under these policies in some countries, including the United States.

None of this matters to those favoring such programs. Affirmative action is symbolic, it is a political trophy of victory, a demonstration of clout for minority "leaders" and it "makes a statement" for the whole countercultural left. Who cares whether it works?

ASSUMPTIONS BEHIND AFFIRMATIVE ACTION

WITH AFFIRMATIVE ACTION SUDDENLY coming under political attack from many directions, and with even liberals backing away from it, we need to question not only its underlying assumptions but also what some of the alternatives are.

At the heart of the affirmative action approach is the notion that statistical disparities show discrimination. No dogma has taken a deeper hold with less evidence—or in the face of more massive evidence to the contrary.

A recent story in the "Wall Street Journal" revealed that more than four-fifths of all the doughnut shops in California are owned by Cambodians. That is about the same proportion as blacks among basketball stars. Clearly, neither of these disparities is due to discrimination against whites.

Nor are such disparities new or peculiar to the United States. In medieval Europe, most of the inhabitants of the towns in Poland and Hungary were neither Poles nor Hungarians. In nineteenth-century Bombay, most of the shipbuilders were Parsees, a minority in Bombay and less than one percent of the population of India.

In twentieth-century Australia, most of the fishermen in the port of Freemantle came from two villages in Italy. In southern Brazil, whole industries were owned by people of German ancestry and such crops as tomatoes and tea have been grown predominantly by people of Japanese ancestry.

Page after page—if not book after book—could be filled with similar statistical disparities from around the world and down through history. Such disparities have been the rule, not the exception. Yet our courts have turned reality upside down and treated what happens all over this planet as an anomaly and what is seldom found anywhere—proportional representation—as a norm.

Why are such disparities so common? Because all kinds of work require particular skills, particular experience, particular locations and particular orientations. And none of these things is randomly distributed.

Local demagogues who thunder against the fact that Koreans run so many stores in black ghettoes merely betray their ignorance when they act as if this were something strange or unusual. For most of the merchants in an area to be of a different race or ethnicity from their customers has been common for centuries in Southeast Asia, Eastern Europe, West Africa, the Caribbean, Fiji, the Ottoman Empire and numerous other places.

When German and Jewish merchants moved into Eastern Europe in the Middle Ages, they brought with them much more experience in that occupation than that possessed by local Eastern European merchants, who were often wiped out by the new competition.

Even when the competition takes place between people who are racially and ethnically identical, all kinds of historical, geographical and other circumstances can make one set of these people far more effective in some activities than the others.

Mountain people have often lagged behind those on the plains below, whether highland Scots versus lowland Scots or the Sinhalese in the highlands of Sri Lanka versus the Sinhalese on the plains. The Slavs living along the Adriatic coast in ports like Dubrovnik were for centuries far more advanced than Slavs living in the interior, just as coastal peoples have tended to be more advanced than peoples of the interior hinterlands in Africa or Asia.

Some disparities of course have their roots in discrimination. But the fatal mistake is to infer discrimination whenever the statistical disparities exceed what can be accounted for by random chance. Human beings are not random. They have very pronounced and complex cultural patterns.

These patterns are not unchanging. But changing them for the better requires first acknowledging that "human capital" is crucial to economic advancement. Those who make careers out of attributing disparities to the wickedness of other people are an obstacle to the development of more human capital among the poor.

There was a time, as late as the mid-nineteenth century, when Japan lagged far behind the western industrial nations because it was lacking in the kind of human capital needed in a modern economy. Importing western technology was not enough, for the Japanese lacked the knowledge and experience required to operate it effectively.

Japanese workmen damaged or ruined machinery when they tried to use it. Fabrics were also ruined when the Japanese tried to dye them without understanding chemistry. Whole factories were badly designed and had to be reconstructed at great cost.

What saved the Japanese was that they recognized their own backwardness—and worked for generations to overcome it. They did not have cultural relativists to tell them that all cultures are equally valid or political activists to tell them that their troubles were all somebody else's fault. Nor were there guilt-ridden outsiders offering them largess.

Affirmative action has been one of the great distractions from the real task of self-development. When it and the mindset that it represents passes from the scene, poorer minorities can become the biggest beneficiaries, if their attention and efforts turn toward improving themselves. Unfortunately, a whole industry of civil rights activists, politicians and miscellaneous hustlers has every vested interest in promoting victimhood, resentment and paranoia instead.

END IT, DON'T MEND IT

"MEND IT, DON'T END IT!" IS THE LATEST SLOGAN by defenders of affirmative action, from Jesse Jackson to Bill Clinton. Yet everything about the history of affirmative action, both in this country and overseas, says that the idea of mending it is completely illusory.

The very reason why affirmative action exists at all in the United States is that laws about "equal opportunity" were changed, by verbal sleight-of-hand, into preferences and quotas by the bureaucracies and the courts. The related practice of "race-norming" test results to inflate the scores of minority applicants likewise arose furtively, without either legislative authorization or judicial mandate.

Even the ability to discuss the issues openly has been undermined by redefinition of the word "quota" to create a distinction without a difference between it and a "goal." College admissions directors routinely deny that they have quotas while saying that they want "representation" of "diverse" groups.

In short, three decades of dishonesty should be ample time for us to understand that good-faith application of standards cannot be expected if any opening at all is left for bringing back preferences and quotas by the back door. That is the door they have always used.

A whole class of affirmative action officials are not going to disappear from government, academia or the corporate world unless what they do is plainly outlawed. The whole mindset that has been spawned will not disappear unless it is frustrated by law at every turn.

Even a newsletter for a scholarly organization like the American Historical Association has featured a whining essay seeking special treatment for minority professors of history, on grounds of the "stress" and "pressure" they are under. According to the AHA's *Perspectives* newsletter, such stress and pressure "imperils the sociological and psychological balance of minority scholars." Worse yet, these were not just the spontaneous outpourings of one writer. The editor of the newsletter noted that this article "was solicited by the AHA's Committee on Minority Historians."

This kind of stuff is not going to go away. It is going to have to be killed and a stake driven through its heart. You cannot have a little bit of preferences any more than you can have a little bit of pregnancy.

The illusion that preferences can be doled out in carefully measured amounts has been disproven, not only all across the United States, but all around the world. In Britain, India, Pakistan and Malaysia, for example, preferential programs were put in place with the proviso that they would be "temporary." Far from declining over time, they have expanded to include more groups, more benefits and more fields of endeavor.

At one time, the argument was made in academia that affirmative action meant nothing more than "special outreach" to minority high school students to get them to apply to colleges where they might not have felt welcome before. After that, this argument went, they would be judged by the same standards and treated the same as everybody else.

Nothing of the sort has happened. Not only are there double standards in admissions, there are often double standards as to what kinds of behavior would be tolerated. Harvard's David Riesman has also written of "affirmative grading."

None of this is peculiar to the United States. Double standards of university admissions exist in Fiji, New Zealand, Nigeria, China, and the Central Asian republics of the former Soviet Union—among other places. What we call "race-norming" of test scores exists in Sri Lanka, where it is called "standardization" of disparate scores earned by Sinhalese and Tamil students. Double standards of grading have been institutionalized in Malaysia.

The kinds of attitudes found in the AHA newsletter are likewise common around the world, where recipients of preferential treatment develop a sense of entitlement. As a group spokesman said in India: "Are we not entitled to jobs just because we are not as qualified?" A Nigerian spoke of "the tyranny of skills." Backlashes against affirmative have been as widespread as the preferences themselves, and have ranged from social polarization in many countries to repeated outbreaks of lethal riots in India to decades of civil war in Sri Lanka.

Those who say, "Mend it, don't end it," assume a degree of control which simply does not exist. Once you have opened the floodgates, the water goes where it will. The only question is whether you are going to close those floodgates.

GRIM LESSONS OF HISTORY

DESPITE UNENDING PRETENTIOUS CHATTER about "multiculturalism," most of what is actually done in the name of multicultural studies is incredibly provincial. It is even Eurocentric, in the sense of being focussed on discrediting Western civilization, both directly and by inflating the intellectual and moral achievements of other societies.

A foreign culture need only claim to be spiritual in order to be praised for its spirituality. Women may be killed over their dowries in India and mob violence among various Indian social groups may take more lives than the worst race riots in the history of the United States, and yet it is Americans who will be called materialistic and violent—and urged to learn from such spiritual and pacific peoples as those of India.

The "diversity" of the multiculturalists is like the diversity of the Clinton administration, with its black lawyers, white lawyers, female lawyers, and Hispanic lawyers. In the academic world, diversity means black leftists, white leftists, female leftists, and Hispanic leftists. Demographic diversity conceals ideological conformity.

Despite the prostitution of "multicultural diversity" to hidden agendas, an honest examination of other societies and other periods of history could provide valuable insights into our own times and our own society.

A businessman from Bombay explained to me some years ago that, when he wants to use more electricity, he has to get prior approval from government bureaucrats. It is by no means sufficient that he can pay for the electricity or even demonstrate a productive use for it. He must submit reports on how he operates his business in general, including its personnel hiring practices. Only if the bureaucrats approve the way he runs his business will he get more electricity.

This is only one of innumerable stifling bureaucratic restrictions on business in India, which may help explain why Indians are so prosperous in so many other countries around the world, but so poor in India itself. If India could bring home the vast entrepreneurial, scientific, and other talent among its own people living in the United States, Fiji, Malaysia, and other countries, this would represent far more financial capital and human capital than all the foreign aid programs put together.

Much the same story could be told of the 30 million overseas Chinese who are prospering from Singapore to San Francisco, and from the Caribbean to London, while the population of China is still struggling to escape from poverty. In China, at least, there is a belated recognition by the Communist leadership that government controls have squelched the very productivity they were intended to create.

Marxist dogma has not prevented the Chinese regime from pulling out of a government-run medical system, even though liberal dogma in Washington remains convinced that this is the way to go. The Chinese have seen the past, and it fails.

Price controls have been tried on every inhabited continent and for 4,000 years of recorded history. Few policies have been tried among more races or in so many different cultural settings. Yet the results have been remarkably similar.

People went hungry in 18th century France and in 20th century Africa when food prices were controlled by the government. Housing shortages have developed from Hong Kong to Berkeley in the wake of rent control. There is indeed much that we could learn from studying other peoples and their history, if only we would.

The grand dogma of our times, that groups would be evenly represented in institutions and activities in the absence of discrimination, would collapse like a house of cards from a study of societies around the world.

People of the same race, religion and language have differed radically according to whether they lived on the flatlands or in the highlands, whether in Scotland or Ceylon. People from the interior hinterlands have differed equally greatly from coastal peoples, whether in Africa or the Balkans. Nomads have differed from peasants, and both from fishermen.

People whose cultures evolved in the struggle for survival in the stark regions of the Mediterranean have for centuries had patterns of frugality unheard of among peoples whose cultures evolved in the plush tropical lands of Southeast Asia. "Fish in the water, rice on the land" is a saying from Thailand, but it is hard to imagine such casual assumptions of abundance developing in the Mediterranean.

In the light of this history, who would expect all the groups in multi-ethnic societies to be evenly represented in all sorts of endeavors? Only the intelligentsia and those who take their dogmas seriously.

Much valuable knowledge could be gained from an honest study of "multicultural diversity," if that has not become a contradiction in terms.

WRONG ANSWERS
OR WRONG QUESTIONS?

MUCH OF THE CURRENT UPROAR about IQ differences between blacks and whites does not get down to the rock-bottom question: What is there to explain? The average score of blacks on IQ tests in the United States is about 85, compared to a national average of 100. Is that unusual? No. It is not.

A variety of groups of various ancestries have had IQs of 85 at various times and places. Many European immigrant groups had IQs of 85 (or lower) during the era of the First World War. These included immigrants of Greek, Portuguese, Slovak, Spanish, and Polish ancestries. The results of the mass testing of American soldiers during the war led Carl Brigham (creator of the Scholastic Aptitude Test) to conclude that the results "disprove the popular belief that the Jew is highly intelligent."

Today, Jewish IQs are consistently above the national average. In other words, IQ scores not only differ among groups, they differ for the same group at different times. American soldiers as a whole scored significantly higher on mental tests in World War II than in World War I, even though there was very little immigration between the two wars to change the genetic makeup of the country.

None of this is peculiar to the United States. Whole countries around the world have improved their performances on mental tests over a period of a generation. As for differences between groups within the same country, these have been as common elsewhere as in the United States. These have included differences between Sephardic and Ashkenazic Jews in Israel, Catholics and Protestants in Ireland, and differences between English-speaking and Gaelic-speaking children in the Hebrides.

Even among illiterate groups from India, Africa and elsewhere, differences have been as great on non-reading tests as the differences between other groups whose varying performances might be thought to be due to education. But the same differences occur where none of the groups has had any education.

At one time, it was thought that racial segregation and discrimination was responsible for black-white differences in the South. But Jewish and Puerto Rican children sitting side-by-side in the same school in New York had even larger differences on IQ tests, as did Mexican American and Japanese American children attending the same schools in California.

If neither education nor genetics can account for many of these differences, what does? I don't know. It is a phrase that should be used more often. It might well replace the phrase, "Well, what is the answer?"

On innumerable issues, we don't know the answers. No small part of the social degeneration in this country over the past 30 years has resulted from the anointed presuming or pretending to know answers that could be applied through government programs. Just think of how many violent criminals have been turned loose on the streets because of fashionable theories, unsubstantiated by any evidence, and often contradicted by such evidence as exists.

A large and largely wasteful expenditure of energy and emotion has gone into rival explanations of statistical disparities. It is widely assumed that such disparities are unusual and therefore require some special, if not sinister, explanation.

In reality, large statistical disparities among groups are the rule rather than the exception, in countries around the world. In Brazil's state if São Paulo, more than 90 percent of the tomatoes have been grown by people of Japanese ancestry. In Malaysia, half the pilots in the air force were from the Chinese minority. In czarist Russia, 40 percent of the army's high command came from the German minority that was one percent of the country's population.

In the race and IQ controversy, we have spent an enormous amount of time, energy and bitter emotion disputing the cause of a phenomenon which both sides often treat as something very unusual, for which there must be some unique explanation, whether that explanation is genes or "society."

This is not to say that the consequences of test score differences do not matter. They can matter greatly at any given time and they matter more and more over time, as technology advances. People who have entirely different theories about test score differences should nevertheless be agreed on the consequences.

Unfortunately, too many people have too much vested interest in particular theories and dogmas to expect rational discussions to become the norm on this subject any time soon. Moreover, the National Education Association and other elements of the education establishment have too much vested interest in maintaining public schools as places devoted to the protecting the jobs of mediocrities (and worse) to expect them to turn these schools into places devoted to raising the educational standards of American children.

Unfortunately, those standards are so low, whether by past standards or by the standards of other countries today, that American youngsters of many different backgrounds are performing far below their potential. The question as to what the ultimate limits of that potential might be are today academic, in the worst sense of the word.

ALIEN NATION AND THE BELL CURVE

PETER BRIMELOW MAY BECOME the Charles Murray of immigration, even if his book *Alien Nation* never sells as many copies as *The Bell Curve*. Like Murray, Brimelow has presented a lot of unwelcome facts that lead to even more unwelcome conclusions on an emotionally charged subject.

The taboos against saying a discouraging word about immigration are second only to the taboos surrounding race. In both cases, this not only leads to policies based on false assumptions and emotional rhetoric, it puts an enormous leverage in the hands of racist demagogues, who may seem to be the only people talking straight, instead of in lofty rhapsodies about "diversity."

Brimelow is not a demagogue but neither is he as disciplined in his writing as Charles Murray. Still, he says a lot of important things that you are not likely to hear from other sources.

Where else will you learn that diseases that were virtually extinct in the United States—tuberculosis, leprosy, measles, cholera, and malaria—have been re-introduced into this country by immigrants? Where else will you learn that people who just crossed the border are eligible for preferential treatment under affirmative action policies which have been sold politically as ways of redressing the wrongs of history to people's ancestors in America?

Where else will you learn that refugees stay on welfare longer than either native-born Americans or other kinds of immigrants? Where else will you learn that some immigrants—mostly from Southeast Asia—go on welfare ten times as often as immigrants from Western European countries like Britain and Germany?

Where else will you learn of the organized criminal activities of Soviet emigres or immigrants from Nigeria?

Written in places in a more rambling and self-indulgent style than
The Bell Curve, Brimelow's *Alien Nation* nevertheless has much
more hard logic to it than most of the pro-immigration literature. First
of all, he rejects the notion that it is somehow morally wrong to be
selective as to who gets in and restrictive as to how many are let in
altogether. In short, he rejects the citizen-of-the-world posture of
those who think that borders are arbitrary things that should be dis-
solved by pretty talk.

Brimelow proceeds from the premise that a society needs bonds
to hold it together and that a common culture and even a common
race may be part of those bonds. The case that a common culture is
necessary is stronger than the case that a common race is necessary.
Most Americans do not regard native-born Japanese Americans or
Chinese Americans as foreign, as shown by the high rates of intermarriage of both groups with the white population and the fact that
neither group is confined to ethnic enclaves any more.

It may be worth noting that a 1992 study which showed blacks
being turned down for mortgage loans more often than whites also
showed whites being turned down more often than Asians. White
hegemony seems to matter less to most Americans than either
Brimelow or many liberals think.

That is very different from saying that most Americans want to
see this country Balkanized by programs designed to keep foreigners foreign in the name of "bilingualism" or "multiculturalism." The
fact that so many of these programs feature fundamental opposition
to the values and traditions of this country makes them all the more
dangerous as instruments in the hands of people with ideological
axes to grind.

These ideologues are not necessarily members of minority
groups themselves. Many are native-born middle class and affluent
white Americans, using immigrants as mascots to symbolize their
countercultural values. Their net effect is to raise both the social and
the financial costs of absorbing immigrants, thereby creating more
public opposition to immigration.

Neither immigrants nor other mascots of the anointed necessarily benefit from their patronage.

The tragedy and the farce of American immigration policy is painfully brought out in *Alien Nation*. Nothing that would be effective in securing our borders is acceptable to the ideologues or to the media pundits whom they have either captured or morally intimidated into silence.

The negative facts that Brimelow brings out against immigration and immigrants are, of course, not the only facts that matter. However, there is little danger that the positive contributions of immigrants will be overlooked in the present atmosphere where "diversity" has become a magic word that is supposed to trump all arguments.

What we need is a real debate about immigration between those who deal in facts and logic. Professor Julian Simon of the University of Maryland would be the best advocate of a pro-immigration policy. Peter Brimelow's *Alien Nation* makes him a top choice for the contrary position.

Can the television networks find time for a serious debate on this subject, in between the sit-coms and the O.J. Simpson trial?

SQUEAMISH WORDS AND DYING BABIES

WITH ALL THE THINGS THAT WERE once taboo now being talked about on nationwide television, there are other things that we are very squeamish about. One of these is the high infant mortality rate among blacks.

Storm clouds of "racism" charges hang over any discussion of any social problems among blacks. But as Charles Murray, among others, has demonstrated, similar problems occur in Europe where similar policies affect whites. Swedes are about as white as you can get, but their illegitimacy rates are close to those of blacks in the United States.

Welfare policies which affect primarily low-income groups like blacks in the United States affect a far wider portion of the population in Sweden, undermining traditional families there as well.

Murray's research on the British underclass shows patterns strikingly similar to those of people living in America's housing projects. Dr. Michael Bernstam of the Hoover Institution has shown how various welfare state policies in the Soviet Union led to large numbers of abandoned "orphans" whose parents were in fact alive and well.

A new study of infant mortality rates in the District of Columbia by Professor Nicholas Eberstadt of Harvard and the American Enterprise Institute once more demonstrates that problems which plague a particular race at a particular time are not necessarily due to race, as such—or to poverty for that matter.

In addition to being the murder capital of the world, Washington also has the highest rate of infant mortality in the country. Since a majority of the population of D. C. is black, some will automatically assume that this is due to poverty, race, racism, lack of "access" to medical care, poor education, and all the rest of the familiar litany of welfare-state liberals.

In reality, other black communities with more poverty, less education, and not nearly as much access to medical care have lower infant mortality rates than those in Washington.

The average income of blacks living in the District of Columbia is much higher than the average income of blacks in the country as a whole. Indeed, it is higher than the average income of whites in Utah and Idaho.

Whether measured by physicians or hospital beds available per capita, Washingtonians have more access to medical care than most other people around the country.

Professor Eberstadt has performed a great public service by getting away from the usual comparisons of blacks and whites, where all differences end up being attributed to racism, history, poverty or the other usual suspects. His research shows that blacks living in Detroit have more than twice as high an unemployment rate as blacks in D. C., higher poverty rates than Washington blacks—and yet the infant mortality rate is lower in Detroit.

What is unique about Washington are the large number of babies born underweight—a condition that puts their survival in jeopardy. Blacks in no other state have such a high incidence of low birth-weight babies.

What makes it so hard for the intelligentsia—black or white—to come to grips with facts like these is that their whole vision of the world is one in which people are the victims of circumstances beyond their control. The very thought that people's own behavior may have something to do with their misfortunes is a threat to the whole house of cards of the modern welfare state.

Nowhere is that welfare state more in operation than in the District of Columbia—and nowhere does it promote more irresponsible behavior with deadly consequences.

While prenatal care is available, some mothers don't bother to get it. Again, comparing only blacks with other blacks, those mothers who don't bother to get prenatal care are twice as likely to smoke, and six times as likely to drink, as those who do. The prenatal care is not what makes the difference. It is just a symptom of a set of attitudes.

Although Professor Eberstadt doesn't mention it, Mexican Americans receive even less prenatal care than blacks, and yet have lower infant mortality rates than either blacks or whites. It is attitudes and behavior, not prenatal care, that is crucial.

Poverty among blacks in Washington is not nearly as highly cor-related with the infant mortality rate as is the incidence of illegiti-macy. Obviously, babies aren't dying because their parents don't have marriage licenses. Again, this is only a symptom of attitudes and behavior.

A different study recently showed that, among black married couples where the husband and wife both worked full-time, the poverty rate was 2 percent. No, that's not a misprint: 98 percent of such black couples were above the poverty level. Again, a marriage license is not magic. It is just a symptom of certain attitudes and be-havior that make an enormous difference.

Nor is this pattern confined to blacks. As more and more whites succumb to the social degeneracy of the welfare state era, their illegitimacy rate has increased five-fold since the early 1960s—and such whites are also having more low-birthweight babies.

Whether for blacks or whites, blaming infant mortality on a lack of "access" to medical care or "parenting skills" is blindly refusing to recognize that personal responsibility is still the key. Where government policies undermine personal responsibility, the results are literally deadly.

SOCIAL CLASSES IN THE BLACK COMMUNITY

WHIST WAS A CARD GAME PLAYED by the British upper classes in the 18th century, but today it is almost exclusively confined to working class blacks in the United States. Back in the 1960s, when blacks first appeared on the Cornell University campus in significant numbers, I concluded a discussion with a black woman who ran the minority students program there by saying:

"Well, now that there are so many other blacks on campus, maybe I can get a game of bid whist going some time."

"I play bridge," she said coldly. She was making a statement about class.

Class differences within in the black community are almost directly the opposite of how they are conceived in the media, when media people are aware of such differences at all. The civil rights establishment has traditionally been the preserve of people from the black middle class, while most of their critics within the black community—the so-called "black conservatives"—have come from a working class background.

Justice Clarence Thomas' humble origins are of course well known, but Walter Williams, Tony Brown, and many other "black conservatives" have similar origins. Such patterns of ideological and social class differences go all the way back to the days of Booker T. Washington and W. E. B. DuBois.

Booker T. Washington rose from poverty, while his more militant rival DuBois grew up in a predominantly white, middle class New England community. Washington moved easily among rural and working class blacks, and talked to them in a language they readily understood, while the aristocratic DuBois was at home only with the elite, whether black or white.

One measure of DuBois' aloofness was that he usually said not a word when he went to a black barbershop for a haircut. DuBois lived at 409 Edgecombe Avenue, when that was Harlem's most prestigious address, a building with uniformed doormen and a fancy entrance. As a teenager, I delivered groceries there—through the service entrance.

A recent parallel to the Washington-DuBois social difference is that of Thurgood Marshall and Clarence Thomas in the Supreme Court, where blacks working in the building have established a rapport with Justice Thomas that they never had with Justice Marshall.

Ironically, white liberals in the media and elsewhere are quick to assume that blacks who criticize the welfare state are middle class people who don't understand what it is like to live in the ghetto. Often, when confronted with the reality, they are unchastened by being proved dead wrong and then proceed to assume that these "black conservatives" must have "sold out" in order to get ahead.

While some people in all groups do in fact sell out in one way or another, nobody sells out to the lowest bidder. For blacks, the real money is to be made on the other end of the political spectrum, among liberals.

When Clarence Thomas had to reveal his net worth, as part of the Supreme Court confirmation process, it came to less than half of what some of the black civil rights leaders make every year. Once, when I was invited to meet with one of these leaders in his hotel suite,

I was amazed to see the opulence of his quarters, which included a spiral staircase leading from his downstairs rooms to the upstairs rooms in the suite.

There is no money to be made advocating that government social programs be cut or eliminated. Even if you convince people to do it, they don't need your help to carry out the reductions. It is when you advocate more government programs that there is money to be made running those programs, researching those programs and serving as a consultant to those programs.

There is also no great demand for black conservatives to speak on college campuses. But Anita Hill or Louis Farrakhan can command five-figure fees to give talks on campuses from coast to coast.

Not only money, but power and influence as well, are more readily available to blacks on the political left. A couple of years ago, a professor of English at a well-known elite college suggested that his institution make an offer to Shelby Steele to join its faculty. However, because Steele has written critically about affirmative action and the victim mentality, the professor was told that the campus black caucus would veto the appointment.

"Wait a minute," he said, "I meant an appointment in the *English* department, not Black Studies. Steele is an English professor." The black caucus would still veto the appointment, he was told.

Serious discussions of the racial and social policies of this country require all the different viewpoints possible. Yet those with a virtual monopoly in the media and in academia have every incentive to maintain that monopoly. The claim to be speaking for the whole black community is part of the process of safeguarding their monopoly. So is discrediting anyone who disagrees.

A NEW AMERICAN DILEMMA

NOT SINCE GUNNAR MYRDAL'S CLASSIC, *An American Dilemma*, just over half a century ago, has any book looked so searchingly at the role of race in American society as Dinesh D'Souza's mew book, *The End of Racism*. Like Myrdal, D'Souza is a foreigner, which gives him the advantage of an outsider's perspective. Also like Myrdal, D'Souza has produced a huge, fact-filled book and examined a wide spectrum of ideas about race against the background of those facts.

Virtually every viewpoint on American race relations gets a hearing in *The End of Racism*—from Al Sharpton and Jesse Jackson to white supremacist hate groups. D'Souza gives them all enough rope to hang themselves and then begins analyzing the facts.

The central theme of this book is that "most of our basic assumptions about racism and civil rights are either wrong or obsolete." D'Souza also demonstrates the enormous importance of underlying, unstated and hence unexamined presuppositions. He traces back to Franz Boas in the 1920s, and his many students and prominent disciples since then, the notion that all cultures are equally valid, that they can only be different but not better or worse.

While cultural relativism may seem to be only an abstract academic doctrine, it has become a key "social science" dogma that has wreaked havoc in racial policy and racial attitudes, from the courtrooms to the halls of Congress to street corner demagogues.

If cultural relativism is correct, then intergroup differences in rewards or achievements can only be due to discrimination or genetic differences in ability. Since cultural relativism began in reaction against racial superiority theories, its rejection of both cultural and genetic causes of intergroup differences leaves only "society" to blame for disparities in income or "representation" in various occupations or institutions.

Although the civil rights movement and the civil rights laws initially sought only equal opportunity, the underlying assumptions of cultural relativism meant that equal opportunity should produce more or less equal results. When this did not happen, the consequence was not a reexamination of this dogma, but instead a proliferation of inherently untestable theories about subtle, hidden, or even unconscious racism—all used to justify affirmative action preferences and quotas.

On the basis of this doctrine, people and institutions began to be presumed guilty in courts of law when their statistics did not match the presuppositions of the zeitgeist. A whole class of people, whom D'Souza calls "the race merchants," came into existence to exploit this way of thinking—or of not thinking—in the courts, in the corporations, in academia and elsewhere.

If one culture was as good as another, then complaints about broken homes or counterproductive behavior and attitudes were all just "perceptions" by observers whose cultural biases needed to be re-educated out of them. Learned professors in leading universities began to accept—or worse yet, to "understand"—both words and deeds of sadistic savagery, as civilized standards degenerated in urban ghettos.

Despite its title, *The End of Racism* does not argue that racism has in fact ended. Instead, it argues that the explanatory power of racism is very weak when put to the test, and that it now serves largely as a distraction from the hard work of dealing with other factors behind very real problems. Moreover, D'Souza sees the ever more elastic definition of "racism" as both escapism and cynical exploitation by racial activists.

"Publicly inconsolable about the fact that racism continues," D'Souza says, "these activists seem privately terrified that it has abated." There is such a vested interest in racism that even independent scholars and writers "are incredulous and even angry" when informed of such things as the declining membership of the Ku Klux Klan and similar racist organizations.

This is a heartbreaking book, because the truth is heartbreaking. The fantasies and frauds of Afrocentric education, the cynical promotion of paranoia and polarization by "the race merchants," and the savage and barbaric crimes of ghetto hoodlums against their own people are just part of the grim and bitter picture painted with meticulous care by D'Souza, who says, "no good is achieved by dressing these pathologies in sociological cant."

Those who cave in to this cant, including some of America's leading corporations, come in for condemnation as well. But *The End of Racism* is more than a series of moral judgments and policy prescriptions. Above all, it is a thorough reappraisal of race and racism in America today. It may not be pleasant reading, but it is must reading.

SINGLING OUT JEWS

NOTHING REPRESENTS MORE OF A TRIUMPH of hope over experience than an attempt to have a rational discussion of racial issues. Nevertheless, recent controversies about anti-Semitic speakers accusing Jews of being slave traders on television, and on college campuses across the country, raise painful questions that have to be addressed.

Blacks and Jews are by no means the only peoples implicated in discussions of slavery. The whole tragic history of slavery has been ideologically distorted beyond recognition, even before the recent demagogic vogue of charging Jews with trading blacks in bondage.

One symptom of this distortion is that many people think automatically of blacks in the antebellum South when slavery is mentioned. Yet Brazil alone imported more than six times as many slaves from Africa as the United States did, and the Islamic countries imported more than the entire Western Hemisphere.

Africa, however, has not been unique as a source of slaves. Slavery has existed virtually everywhere that human beings have existed. Professor David Eltis of Queens University in Canada, a leading scholar in this field, says that slavery was "universal" until very recently as history is measured, that "few peoples in the world have not constituted a major source of slaves at one time or another."

The very word "slave" derives from the Slavs, who were enslaved longer than the entire history of the United States, and about twice as long as blacks were enslaved in North America.

Despite the universality of this hideous institution and its victims, books and articles on slavery are overwhelmingly about slavery in the United States, or at most about slavery in the Western Hemisphere. This is true of both academic studies and popular literature. Many use this universal institution as a moral indictment, selectively applied to Western civilization.

Ironically, it was Western civilization which eventually destroyed slavery around the world, during the era when European imperialism reached every continent. Even autonomous nations which abolished slavery usually did so under pressure from the West or in order to avoid the national embarrassment of being regarded as uncivilized by the West. But this whole epic story—perhaps the biggest moral achievement in history—remains largely untold, because it does not fit the ideological vision of the intelligentsia.

On a subject where such ideological distortion has been the rule rather than the exception, it was perhaps inevitable that someone would take it a step further and single out Jews as responsible for the enslavement and trading of Africans. But when it came to enslaving human beings and trading them like cattle, blacks did it, whites did it, Jews did it, Gentiles did it. There was slavery in China and Russia and in the island paradise of Bali.

If this presents an ugly picture of the human race, so be it. But to talk about Jews trading slaves is like saying that white people have toenails. It is true enough in itself, but grossly misleading if it suggests that non-whites do not have toenails.

During the long era of slavery, going back thousands of years and extending around the world, merchant peoples in general traded slaves along with other merchandise. Venetians, Greeks and Jews did so in Europe, the overseas Chinese in Southeast Asia, the Arabs in Africa and the Middle East, as well as various African tribes, among many other peoples in many other places.

None of those who are trying to whip up Americans of African ancestry against Jews points out that the Arabs were among the principal enslavers and traders of Africans, while Jews were much more likely to be trading Slavs in Medieval Europe and around the Mediterranean. No doubt diligent research can turn up cases of Jews holding or trading black slaves in the Western Hemisphere, but blacks themselves did the same thing in the Caribbean and in New Orleans and Charleston, among other places. Nobody's hands are completely clean.

Even if the discussion of slavery is arbitrarily restricted to the enslavement of black people, Jews come far down the list of those involved. They cannot compare with the number of Africans who held fellow-Africans in bondage in Africa, not even counting those who sold their black brothers to the white man.

Most Jews were in no position to trade slaves, and had all that they could do to survive the persecutions to which they were themselves subjected. But leading scholars—both Jews and Gentiles—affirm that Jews were not exempt from taking part in this global trade.

The singling out of Jews and the implication that they had some special role in the enslavement of Africans is an outrage rightly being condemned, though not by enough people. Unfortunately, it is only a further extension of the pervasive selective history and selective moral indignation that has long marked the discussion of slavery and other issues, even in "respectable" circles.

"GIVING BACK"

WHY IS EVERYONE SO SURPRISED that Nation of Islam leader Louis Farrakhan has called Jews "bloodsuckers"? He and his followers have called them this—and worse—before. What his growing acceptance among black "leaders" has meant is the mainstreaming of hate.

Black Muslim spokesmen have given anti-Semitic speeches on leading college campuses all across the country. They have been liberally rewarded (in both senses of the word) for doing so by the colleges that pay them generous lecture fees.

Jews are not the only group called "bloodsuckers" by Farrakhan. He includes Koreans, Vietnamese and others who run businesses in black ghettos and who "suck the value of its life without returning anything."

This whole notion of returning something to the community is not unique to Farrakhan or the Black Muslims. You hear it all the time from all sorts of people who talk loftily about "giving something back" in exchange for one's own good fortune. It is one of the many signs of the degeneration of the American educational system that such mindless talk is repeated uncritically in so many places.

What is there to "return"? If you took something you were not entitled to, then you shouldn't have taken it in the first place. And if you are entitled to it, why should it be returned? If businesses are being expected to return part of what they earned, are customers being expected to return the merchandise they bought?

Is the argument seriously being made that unusually high profits are being received by those who do business in ghetto communities? Then why are so many businesses leaving and passing up these lucrative profits?

As for the Jews, many of them left long ago, which is why so many Asian and Middle Eastern store owners and other businessmen are found today in ghettos around the country.

None of this makes any sense if you stop and examine it. The great problem is that so few people stop and examine emotional words. This is the Oprah and Donahue generation.

Misconceptions about the role of businesses in general and middleman minorities in particular have been all too common for all too long, even among the intelligentsia. Indeed, some of the worst nonsense has come from people with Ph.D.s.

First of all, there is nothing unusual about people of one racial or ethnic background predominating among the people operating in a community whose residents are from a different racial or ethnic background. Greeks and Armenians were the leading businessmen in many Turkish communities during the days of the Ottoman Empire. People from China and India have dominated much of commerce and industry in Malaysia, as the Lebanese have in West Africa and many other groups in many other places.

The reason is quite simple: Different groups have different kinds of skills. The intelligentsia may live in a never-never land of the mind where statistical disparities are suspicious and sinister but such disparities have been the rule, not the exception, in countries around the world.

Whether it is basketball or brain surgery, different groups are seldom equally represented. Race doesn't even have to be involved. Englishmen from different parts of England settled in different parts of the United States and lived very different lifestyles, producing very different results.

Just because you cannot see the differences with the naked eye doesn't mean that they are not there when the groups are physically indistinguishable. For example, the first forty classes at Harvard had only one student named Edward and it was nearly two centuries before they had anyone named Patrick.

These were not just flukes. Even though Edward was a very popular name for people from certain parts of England, the descendants of those kinds of people didn't go to Harvard. Patrick was one of the most popular names among those who settled in western Pennsylvania during this era, but the kind of people who lived in western Pennsylvania were not welcome even in eastern Pennsylvania, much less at Harvard.

The real reason why people in the ghettos have so few businesses serving them, and why those businesses often charge high prices and give bad service, is that demagogues, crime, riots, vandalism, and shoplifting have made these places unattractive for most businesses. Back when I was growing up in Harlem, there were plenty of Jewish and other businesses there—so many that none of them dared to given the kind of rotten service that people in the black ghettos have to put up with today.

High prices, often being charged for inferior merchandise and discourteous service, cover higher costs of doing business. Anyone who thinks that what is needed is more demagoguery, more riots, etc., is welcome to continue along that path—if he is prepared to sacrifice another whole generation of blacks in the process.

Maybe we need less marching and more thinking.

CAN INTELLIGENCE BE DISCUSSED INTELLIGENTLY?

THE RECENT DEATH OF PROFESSOR RICHARD J. HERRNSTEIN of Harvard has left Charles Murray to face alone the attacks on the book that he and Herrnstein co-authored, entitled *The Bell Curve*. Since this book is about intelligence tests, all sorts of idiotic attacks can be expected.

Newsweek magazine has already taken the low road by calling this "an angry book." Anybody who wants to know how honestly the mass media deal with issues should just pick up a copy of *The Bell Curve* off a shelf merely long enough to look through a few pages at random to see if he can find anything that could even remotely be called "angry."

This is one of the most sober, responsible, thorough and thoughtful books to be published in years. I don't happen to agree with everything in it, but that is beside the point.

How can we possibly address any of the painful social problems afflicting this country if any attempt to analyze evidence is met by name-calling and cheap attempts at amateur psychoanalysis? Unfortunately, the liberal establishment too often "replaces the intellectual discussion of arguments by the moral extermination of persons," in the words of distinguished French author Jean-Francois Revel.

What we are seeing now is the beginning of a campaign for the moral extermination of Charles Murray, in order to avoid facing the issues he raises and the empirical evidence that he presents.

Ironically, the central thesis of *The Bell Curve*—that heredity plays a role in intelligence—is not seriously disputed among those who have done research in this area. Nor is the average layman likely to find the idea all that startling. It is only among the liberal intelligentsia that this is a subject for controversy and hysteria.

In the prevailing liberal vision, problems are caused by "society" and solutions can be imposed by government. Anything that goes against this vision is fiercely resisted, and anyone who promotes views that question the liberal vision is likely to be demonized.

One of the ways of demonizing Murray is that used by *Newsweek* to tie him and his co-author to age-old attempts to keep blacks down. In reality, "The Bell Curve" says: "It should be no surprise to see (as one does every day) blacks functioning at high levels in every intellectually challenging field."

The book begins by examining the role of I.Q. solely among whites, in order to avoid having the whole discussion get bogged down in inflammatory racial issues. It is Chapter 13 before they even begin discussing "Ethnic Differences in Cognitive Ability."

What Murray and Herrnstein have established up to that point is that I.Q. scores are highly correlated with academic success, with success in high-level careers, and even with success in the most routine jobs and with such things as infant mortality, where the children of low-I.Q. women are far more likely to die in infancy.

Far from being "angry" writers determined to prove some dogma, Murray and Herrnstein examine alternative explanations of many of the things they find, including racial differences in I.Q. scores. That is why the book is so huge. Some of these alternative explanations fall by the wayside when you look at them closely. Others do not.

Newsweek says that Murray and Herrnstein "straddle" or "contradict themselves" when they present alternative ways of looking at the same set of facts. It could also be called intellectual honesty, if such a notion has not gone completely out of fashion.

Facts are complicated and it is not always easy to get them straight. One small but revealing example is that both *The Bell Curve* and the *Newsweek* story about it refer to "psychologist James Flynn." It so happens that I know Jim Flynn and he is not a psychologist. He is chairman of the political science department at the University of Otago in New Zealand.

Professor Flynn's findings about I.Q. scores go counter to some of the conclusions reached by Murray and Herrnstein in *The Bell Curve*. I happen to think that Flynn is right and said so in this column 6 years ago. But the fact that Murray and Herrnstein present his ideas in their book is to their credit.

It is to the discredit of *Newsweek* and others that they do not give the same kind of careful analysis to the ideas—and hard facts— presented in *The Bell Curve*.

PART VI

THE
EDUCATION
SCENE

ANTI-"ELITISM" IN EDUCATION

IT CAUSED TWINGES OF NOSTALGIA when I read about Stuyvesant High School's classes of 1947 and 1948 holding a joint 50th year reunion. I went to New York's Stuyvesant High School but, by 1948, I had dropped out and was getting my education from the school of hard knocks.

The most startling part of the story was that Stuyvesant High School now has an olympic-sized swimming pool. No way could the old and battered school that I went to have such a thing. This was a new and palatial Stuyvesant, at a new location overlooking the Hudson River. The school I went to overlooked the tenements on the lower east side.

Stuyvesant is and was something very unusual in American public schools—a high school that you had to pass a test to get into. Back in my day, only about a third of those who took the test got in. And our junior high school in upper Manhattan limited how many would even be allowed to go take the test.

The Bronx High School of Science used the same test as Stuyvesant, while Brooklyn Tech used an even tougher one. While such schools have always been rare outside of New York, and have come under increasing political pressure to be more "open," even within the city, they provided both the poor and the society with golden opportunities. You could come from the poorest family in town and yet receive a high-quality education that would enable you to go anywhere and compete with the graduates of Exeter or Andover.

The envy-laded concept of "elitism" has been thrown at these and other high-quality schools across the country, and political pressures have been put on them to admit more students without such high academic skills. Seldom do the people who push such notions stop to think that you cannot let everyone go to Stuyvesant without its ceasing to be the kind of school that makes them want to go there.

You cannot teach everyone at the same pace, unless that pace is slowed down to accommodate the lowest common denominator. There are kids who can handle calculus in the tenth grade—and others who struggle with it in college.

Ironically, many so-called minority "leaders" have led the charge to get top-level public schools to admit students on some basis other than academic achievement. Yet no one needs such schools more than poor and disadvantaged children who want to rise to higher levels in the economy and the society.

There may not be a high percentage of minority students who are currently able to take advantage of outstanding high schools. But part of the reason is that the elementary schools in many minority communities have deteriorated so much since the days when I went to P.S. 5 in Harlem. Kids in P.S. 5 in the 1940s had test scores equal to those of white kids in the immigrant neighborhoods on the lower east side.

One revealing statistic is that more black boys went to Stuyvesant in 1938 than in 1983—even though the black population of New York was much smaller in 1938. Moreover, those black kids who did not want to make the long trip from Harlem down to Stuyvesant had some decent high schools available to them closer to home.

In Washington, D. C., the similarly old and battered Dunbar High School has likewise been replaced by a modern building. But the new Dunbar is not even in the same league with the old school that once housed the finest black high school in the nation. Back in the 1930s, Dunbar's all-black student body had test scores above the national average, while going to a rundown school with overcrowded classes.

The old Dunbar turned out the first black general, the first black federal judge, the first black cabinet member, . . . and on and on. More than one-fourth of the Dunbar graduates who later graduated from Amherst College during the period from 1892 to 1954 graduated Phi Beta Kappa. Of the few high-level black military officers in World War II, more than two dozen with ranks of major to brigadier general were Dunbar graduates.

You might think that black political leaders would move heaven and earth to preserve a school like this. But you would be wrong. The Marion Berry generation of "leaders" in Washington have promoted the same class-warfare envy found in the larger society and denounce the very memory of this "elitist" school, whose quality was destroyed overnight back in the 1950s, by turning it into a neighborhood school.

May Stuyvesant and other high schools like it escape the sad fate of Dunbar.

HIGHER EDUCATION AND LOW COMEDY

IF YOU LIKED *Alice in Wonderland,* you will love *The Chronicle of Higher Eductation,* the trade publication of academia. Just one issue—dated the 13th of October, for those who are superstitious—contained stories about professors that make you wonder if academics ever grow up.

In that issue, New York University advertised for a faculty member in the performing arts, for what it called "Gendered Performance." The specific duties of the job include "drag, transvestite performance, queer theories." The university "encourages applications from women and members of minority groups." None of the usual stuff about being an "equal opportunity/affirmative action employer," that we have grown so used to that its internal contradictions no longer bother us.

In what literally became a federal case, a professor at the University of Alabama injected his religious views into a physical exercise class that he taught. When the university told him to stop it, he sued. Eventually, he lost the case but gained tenure, so perhaps it was a stand-off.

Had he injected left-wing ideologies into wholly unrelated subjects like biology or English—as happens routinely on many campuses across the country—he would never even have been warned.

Another federal case arose because a professor who cussed out his students in class ignored warnings to stop it and then sued when he was eventually fired. This case went as far as the U. S. Circuit Court of Appeals, where the prof lost.

This does not mean that mere profanity in the classroom is grounds for firing a professor. It was only the fact that the profanity was directed against students that got the professor in trouble. All across the country, and all up and down the academic pecking order from Harvard to Podunk A & M, four-letter words are O.K. in the classroom under the broad umbrella of "academic freedom."

Professors who go to bed with their students are also covered by "academic freedom," even if they are not covered by anything else. The same issue of *The Chronicle of Higher Education* includes letters from readers responding to an essay by a professor at the University of Massachusetts who says that he has remedied the problem of female students whose virginity was "unnaturally prolonged."

Again, we need have no fear for this professor's job, either for his actions or his subsequent boasts about them. It is very unlikely that his de-flowering of student virgins will add to the congestion of the federal courts.

At Stanford, incidentally, male students can get into all kinds of trouble under a new and vaguely worded "sexual harassment" code, but Stanford professors who go to bed with their students are merely admonished.

Mob rule is also alive and well in academia. The same issue of *The Chronicle of Higher Education* reports on a riot at U.C.L.A. in which students attacked the faculty club. They "broke the club's plate-glass windows, wrecked furniture, and carved graffiti in its walls."

In due course, they were rewarded by the U.C.L.A. administration's promise to add two new professors in Chicano Studies and to exempt ethnic studies programs from any of the cutbacks that might hit such non-relevant subjects as mathematics or economics.

The *Chronicle* also reported on similar events at Berkeley: "Several hundred protesters ran through two campus buildings and pulled fire alarms. No one was arrested."

Note that "protestors" is the politically correct term for rioters, vandals, or storm troopers on campus.

Although these "protestors" are routinely reported as expressing their "rage" or their "anguish," one of the Cornell student leaders may have captured the real spirit more accurately when he said, after various organized acts of vandalism there: "This is very exciting."

One of the reasons we don't hear much about such campus outbursts in the general media, the way we did back in the 1960s, is that they happen too often to be news—and are accepted too supinely to have the drama of conflict.

Experienced academic administrators have also learned how to minimize the number of such episodes by various techniques of pre-emptive surrender. By staying constantly aware of what is most likely to set off the most volatile elements among the students and faculty, administrators know which way to bend academic policy and whose misconduct or outright crimes are to be overlooked.

This game works only because many outside of academia are not even aware that the game is being played. But, before deciding whether to contribute to dear old Alma Mater, it might be well worthwhile to subscribe to *The Chronicle of Higher Education*. You could end up deciding to donate to medical research instead, or to invest the money in the marketplace, where it will help create jobs.

TRAGI-COMIC "EDUCATORS"

AMERICAN EDUCATION WOULD BE COMIC if it were not so tragic in its consequences.

Recently I received a letter from a school teacher, asking for an autographed picture for his class because it would "ultemetly" help his students to have me as a "roll model." Atypical? Let us hope so. But a few years ago a study showed the average verbal Scholastic Aptitude Test score for aspiring teachers to be 389 out of a possible 800.

With American school children repeatedly finishing at or near the bottom on international test comparisons, the response of the education establishment has been to seek ever more non-academic adventures to go off on. Among the latest of these "innovations"— a magic word in the wonderland of educational Newspeak—is something called "outcome-based education." Like so many of the catch phrases that come and go, it means nothing like what it seems to mean.

Education based on outcomes might sound to many people like finally creating a bottom line for schools, teachers and administrators to be judged by. Nothing of the sort. It is yet another way of getting away from academic work and indulging in psychological and ideological indoctrination. This is called advancing beyond "rote learning" and teaching school children to "think." Many in the media gullibly repeat such phrases, without the slightest investigation of what concretely they mean in practice.

When specifics leak out, there is often shock, as there currently is in California, where tests are intruding into students' family lives and sexual experiences, among other things. The parents who first protested were predictably labelled "the religious right," but now even some in the educational establishment itself have begun to express concern. Not long before, parents in Connecticut who objected to film strips of naked couples engaged in sex (both homosexual and

heterosexual) being shown in the local junior high school were labelled "fundamentalists" and "right-wing extremists," even though
they were in fact affluent Episcopalians.

There are all sorts of prepackaged responses to critics of the public schools, of which this was just one. Recently, I got a first-hand
dose of these stereotyped responses when addressing a class of students who are being trained for careers as teachers. They seemed dis-
concerted by the questions I put to them:

"Suppose you are wrong? How would you know? How would
you test for that possibility?"

The very thought that the dogmas they were repeating with such
fervor might be open to question or subject to evidence seemed never
to have occurred to them. This was a far more ominous sign than their
merely being wrong on particular beliefs. How can they teach anybody else to think if they themselves have not reached this elementary level of logic?

By "thinking" too many educators today mean teaching children
to reject traditions in favor of their own emotional responses. Objections to such propaganda programs are called objections to letting
children think. Anything less than a blank check for indoctrination is
called "censorship."

In light of such non-academic activities in our public schools, it
can hardly be surprising that American youngsters do so badly on
academic tests administered to youngsters around the world. Nor is
it surprising that academic work is so readily abandoned for social
experiments, ideological crusades and psychological manipulations
by educators whose own academic performances have long been
shown to be substandard.

It is not uncommon for those few schools with traditional academic programs to have waiting lists of parents who want to get their
children admitted. When admission is on a first-come, first-serve
basis, it is not uncommon for parents to camp out overnight in
hopes of getting their children into institutions that will teach them
substance instead of fluff and politically correct propaganda.

Against this background, recent campaigns for a longer school
day and a longer school year are farcical. If a lack of time is the

problem, why are schools wasting so much time on innumerable non-academic activities? Moreover, there is no amount of additional time that cannot be wasted on similar pursuits.

No small part of the existing problems of the public schools is that the school day is already so long and boring, with so little to challenge the ablest students. Moreover, many average and below-average students who have lost all interest are retained by compulsory attendance laws for years past the point where their presence is accomplishing anything other than providing jobs for teachers.

Despite orchestrated hysteria about "the dropout problem," what many apathetic students most need is a cold dose of reality that they can only get out in the workaday world—not in the never-never land of the public schools.

DAMAGING ADMISSIONS

ANYONE WHO WANTS TO KNOW how college admissions directors at elite institutions think should read the recently published book *Questions and Admissions* by Jean H. Fetter. But, if you want to know why in God's name anyone would think that way, you will have to get some other book by somebody else.

Jean Fetter was dean of admissions at Stanford University from 1984 through 1991. Her book may be the best statement of the prevailing creed in college admissions offices at elite institutions.

Do not expect to learn from Ms. Fetter's book why a student's extracurricular activities in general or "public service" in particular are important considerations in the admissions process, or why "societal injustices" are to be rectified there. She just says they are, as if all right-thinking people already know why.

Questions and Admissions is at its best as a guided tour of the college admissions process. Here we meet the dedicated staff who work incredible hours poring over the application folders, we see the pain of their agonizing choices and the exhilaration they feel at the end, when they conclude that theirs has been a job well done. Then we grieve with their vicissitudes as angry parents and their tearful children demand to know why they were not admitted.

Who knows? There may be a great TV series here. But, for those of us so narrow as to want to know what all this sound and fury signifies, the pickings are very lean.

Ms. Fetter elaborates the "complexities" of the choices facing the admissions committee and the "sensitivity" with which they make those choices, but the book is much less clear on just what it is that they are trying to achieve—and there is absolutely nothing that would enable anyone to test how well they have achieved it.

If—horror of horrors—these wonderfully complex and sensitive people were replaced by a computer, how would we know whether the end results were better or worse? To Ms. Fetter, it may seem axiomatic that the results would be worse. But to those of us old-fashioned enough to want some standard by which to test that empirically, she gives us very little to go on.

Anyone who wants to see these kinds of questions dealt with concretely and straightforwardly would do far better to read *Choosing Elites* by Robert Klitgaard. Professor Klitgaard studied the admissions process at Harvard, which is not very different from that at Stanford, but he did so as an outsider with no axe to grind and no need to obscure or evade.

What Jean Fetter presents as a complexity of the admissions process is too often a confusion of criteria. It is never clear in *Questions and Admissions*—or in other writings by other deans of admissions—whether the admissions office's job is to pick those students with the best prospects of producing the biggest bang for the buck out of their education or to dispense the largess of admissions to the most deserving souls.

Repeatedly the author gives examples of applicants whose outstanding academic achievements reflect privileges not enjoyed by others—and argues that it would be unfair to penalize those others by giving too much weight to such achievements.

Ms. Fetter does not think it would have been right to require Achievement Tests, for example, because "such tests could unfairly penalize disadvantaged students" who, "through no fault of their own" went to high schools that gave them inadequate preparation.

Lest you think that there are double standards at Stanford, Ms. Fetter declares that "my staff and I took pride in our focus on the *individual,* not on any groups or representatives of groups." She rejects "myths" about "purported quotas."

Several pages later, however, we learn that some "categories of applicants receive special consideration" and that "Stanford University is committed to a substantial representation of Blacks, Mexican Americans, and Native American Indians."

In a sense, it is unfair to single out Ms. Fetter for using this kind of double talk, which is standard operating procedure in admissions offices across the country. So too is evasion of brutal statistics on intergroup differences in test scores. As Ms. Fetter puts it, "application of quantitative measures to the selection process at Stanford is ill-founded" because the admissions staff "do not admit by SAT scores and grade-point averages."

Likewise, teams in the National Basketball Association do not hire by height. But, if we discovered that Irish players in the NBA averaged around 5 foot 6 every year, for decades on end, wouldn't we suspect double standards?

Whether in basketball or college admissions or elsewhere, are we to believe that the factors we cannot see are always so lopsidedly in favor of one group that it consistently counterbalances the factors that we can see? Give us a break, lady.

GLIMPSES OF ACADEME

THE CHRONICLE OF HIGHER EDUCATION recently gave us its annual glimpse into the minds of college professors. Perhaps the most salient item, for parents preparing to send their children off to college, was the professors' response to the statement, "The faculty are rewarded for good teaching." Only 13 percent agreed with that statement. There was no "gender gap"; it was 13 percent for both male and female professors.

The professors surveyed were not just from big-name research universities. Research has become the golden idol across most of the academic spectrum. On many campuses, bringing in research money is a precondition for getting tenure. It is not just research but research money that talks, especially to the academic administration, which gets its cut as "overhead" reimbursement.

Although fewer professors declared that their own primary interest was in research, as compared to teaching, they also know which side their bread is buttered on, so most have published in academic journals more than once and 16 percent have published 20 or more times in such journals, not counting their books and monographs.

The *Chronicle of Higher Education's* survey did not get into the quality or relevance of what is published, but editors of leading scholarly journals in various fields have said that much of the research that is done is a waste of time. However, the money received to finance time-wasting research is just as valuable to a college or university as money received to find a cure for fatal diseases.

About two-thirds of all professors spend no more than 12 hours per week in the classroom. This includes 35 percent who spend no more than 9 hours per week in the classroom. A roughly comparable amount of time is spent preparing for classes, but these two activities put together add up to what most people would consider to be a part-time job.

Not all the other time is spent in research. There are also committee meetings and work for clients, for those who are consultants. About 40 percent of the women and 48 percent of the men worked as paid consultants. Then there are off-campus meetings at various watering holes under the general heading of "professional activities."

A recent supplement to *The Chronicle of Higher Education* listed conventions, symposia and conferences for academics for the coming year. This supplement was about the size of a tabloid newspaper, but with much smaller type, so that most of its 40 pages had 5 columns of listings of these academic get-togethers.

Most were in places like the Caribbean or Hawaii and the hotels were typically Hiltons, Sheratons or Hyatts. I did not notice any meetings being held in Gary, Indiana or Newark, New Jersey, nor any meetings in the Motel 6 chain.

As for the quality of students the colleges are getting these days, only 24 percent of professors agreed with the statement, "Faculty feel that most students are well-prepared academically" and only 12 percent agreed that most of the students are "very bright."

These professors were by no means all old-timers, nostalgic for a different world. Fewer than 10 percent of these faculty members received their highest degree before the 1960s. Most received their highest degree within the past 20 years. In other words, the professors consider the students ill-prepared even by the more lax standards of recent times.

The least surprising finding from this survey is that liberalism reigns supreme in academe. Three-quarters of the professors are for a "national health care plan" to "cover everybody's medical costs." However, a statement that the undergraduate curriculum should be based on Western civilization gets only a 53 percent agreement.

Only 28 percent thought it essential or very important to teach students the classic works of Western civilization, while 80 percent thought that colleges should encourage students to get involved in "community service" activities and nearly a third thought that this should be a requirement for graduation.

In other words, Plato and Shakespeare should be optional, but such things as working in a homeless shelter should be pushed or compelled.

Perhaps the most encouraging statistic is that 31 percent of these professors are considering early retirement. On the other hand, it is by no means clear that their replacements will be any better.

BEHIND "PUBLISH OR PERISH"

"PUBLISH OR PERISH: A WELL-LIKED PROFESSOR is Bumped by Rutgers." That was the headline in the *New York Times*.

Perhaps the most surprising thing about the story was that anyone was surprised—or even considered it news. The story was all too familiar. Professor Richard L. Barr had won three awards for his teaching during his six years at Rutgers University and was then told that his contract would not be renewed.

This has happened so often, on so many campuses across the country, that many in academia regard teaching awards as the kiss of death. Two of my college room mates went into teaching and each won teaching awards, one at Harvard and the other at M.I.T. Each was then told that his contract would not be renewed.

A quarter of a century ago, a colleague who had the same experience at Brandeis University referred to the teaching award as "travel money."

From time to time, college and university presidents announce that they are going to restore the balance between teaching and research by giving more emphasis to teaching. This too is usually treated in the media as if it were news. What would be news would be if it happened. Few professors are prepared to jeopardize their careers by depending on such statements—and those who do usually end up paying the price for their naivete.

Although things have been going this way for some decades now, colleges and universities were not always like this from time immemorial. How did they get this way and what can be done about it?

They got this way, in large part, because of the vast sums of money made available for research by federal and state governments. Unlike other social problems whose solutions are said to require more "funding," this is a problem that can be dealt with by budget-cutting.

Medical, scientific and engineering research produce many benefits for the larger society. But English professors writing far-out drivel produce benefits only for English professors trying to publish to keep from perishing. It is hard to imagine how the world would be any worse off, on net balance, if the entire output of the sociology profession over the past 50 years had never been published.

Unfortunately, colleges and universities have become bloated with research money, spawning all sorts of expensive boondoggles and layers of bureaucracy to oversee the boondoggles. To keep all this going, academic institutions have to have the kind of professors who can keep the research money flowing in. Thus means have become ends in themselves—and have sacrificed the original ends of education.

One of the few legitimate points made in defense of publishing requirements is that it is very difficult to make valid assessments of teaching quality. Popularity is not profundity, so there must be some other way to determine whether a professor has "the right stuff." Subjecting his thinking to quality control by others in his profession via the publishing route makes more sense than depending on whether he wows the sophomores three mornings a week. Every campus has its flashy mush heads on the faculty.

However, you do not need a constant stream of articles and books tumbling off the press on the heels of one another, in order to tell whether you have someone with a serious mind or just a clever talker. The argument against Professor Barr at Rutgers—at least what appeared in the news story—was not that he hadn't published anything or that its quality was low, but that his collection of publications was "not so thick as the usual packet for tenure."

If publication is going to be a numbers game, then we need to recognize that Charles Darwin, Adam Smith, and Sir Isaac Newton would never have gotten tenure because they didn't grind it out as fast as an ambitious assistant professor at an Ivy League university today. There is no inherent reason why tenure decisions have to be made the same way for all individuals in all fields and in all institutions. Indeed, there is no inherent reason to have tenure in the first place.

The "academic freedom" argument for tenure gets more and more threadbare as more and more scholars work in think tanks where there is no tenure. The research coming out of these think tanks is at least as independent as that coming out of universities operating under the stultifying conformity of political correctness.

Can academia kick its research addiction cold turkey? Only if those who supply the money learn to "just say no."

EBONICS AND MONEY

THE KEY TO THE TRAGI-COMEDY in Oakland, California, where the school board wants to set up a program on "black English" or "ebonics," is revealed in the board's own resolution, where "special funding" is mentioned. It is the old story: Follow the money.

The massive infusions of federal money which began flowing into the American public schools in the 1960s were followed by a steady decline in test scores, as all sorts of distractions from academic studies were created, in order to have "innovative" and "exciting" programs to attract money from the U. S. Treasury.

This was bad enough for the general population. It was catastrophic for the poorer and less educated segments of the population, for whom education is a must if they are to rise.

With all the fictitious history about the origins of ghetto speech, there is remarkably little interest in the real history of this dialect or in the history of the educational performances of ghetto children in the era before they began receiving the "benefits" of educational "innovation."

Words and phrases like "ain't" or "I be" and "you be" do not come from any African language. They came from the parts of England from which many white Southerners originated. The *Cambridge History of the English Language* pin-points the regions of the British Isles from which words like "chitterlings" or "chittlin's" came or where people said "ain't" and used other terms now thought to be "black English."

In short, what is called "black English" is just as white as any other English. It is a dialect that died out as education and standardization of the language proceeded over the generations.

The claim that having teachers understand this dialect is somehow going to help the abysmal educational level of ghetto schools likewise flies in the face of history. Decades ago, when children in Harlem were being taught in standard English and no one dreamed of any such pretentious nonsense as "ebonics," their test scores were quite comparable to test scores of children in the schools on the lower east side of New York.

Both sets of schools were in working-class neighborhoods where the people had arrived in the city relatively recently—some from Europe and some from the American South. In neither place were the test scores as high as in posh neighborhoods, but neither were they miles below the norms, as they are today.

In December 1941, sixth-grade students in P.S.5 in Harlem (my alma mater) scored 5.2 on tests of word meaning and paragraph meaning. On the lower east side, P.S. 130 scored 5.1 on tests of word meaning and 4.7 on paragraph meaning. Moreover, P.S. 5 was not the highest scoring school in Harlem, nor was P. S. 130 the lowest-scoring school on the lower east side. In some other years, the lower east side school had an edge, but it was only an edge either way.

The city-wide average was 6.0 on both tests, but these recently arrived and poor children were not out of it, by any means.

Many heart-warming stories have been told of the rise of immigrant children from the lower east side in various walks of life. Similar stories could be told of black children from that same era. After all, where did today's black middle class come from, if not from such places? But it would not serve the political purposes of today to tell those stories, when hopelessness and guilt are the themes that get federal grants, so these experiences will likely die with those of us who lived through that era.

Let us understand what an achievement that was. The average black American in 1940 had only six years of schooling. My family was typical in that respect. A great fuss was made over me when I was promoted to the seventh grade, because no one else in our family had ever gone that far.

Most of the parents in Harlem were in no position to help their children speak English, any more than the immigrant parents on the lower east side were. The schools taught them. Teachers did not cater to the students' dialects or spend time trying to "understand" their psyches. There was no federal money to finance myth-makers and hustlers who would in later decades lure educators off into never-never land.

Follow the money if you want to understand what is happening in Oakland and in all too many other places across the country. But follow common sense if you want to see ghetto children get a decent education.

NO COLLEGE PRESIDENT

MY WIFE IS ALWAYS AMAZED WHENEVER I get a letter asking me if I want to be considered as a candidate to be president of some college.

"What are those people smoking?" she asks.

It would be a guarantee of big trouble if I were a college president. First of all, I am not politically correct. I don't go around using all the pious phrases about "diversity" and other cant that are almost obligatory for college presidents.

I think tenure and so-called "faculty self-governance" are two of the biggest mistakes ever made in academia. Tenure turns ordinary professors into little tin gods who do their own thing, instead of doing what they are paid to do. Many turn their classrooms into propaganda centers for their pet ideologies, instead of teaching the subject listed in the catalog.

Some teach about what they happen to be writing about, rather than what is fundamental to the field. Thus a history department may have a course on the history of movies, but no course on the history of France or Germany, and a philosophy department may have no course on logic but several courses on feminist philosophy.

Faculty self-governance would make sense if it meant simply that chemistry teachers, for example, would decide what chemistry courses should be taught and in what sequence. But what it really means is that professors get to make policy on things for which they have no special expertise.

Thus professors of English literature or organic chemistry get to decide whether or not the college's students will be allowed to take R.O.T.C. or whether the university's endowment can be invested on the basis of financial principles or ideological principles.

Some years ago, a trustee at Grove City College said to me emphatically, "Here the faculty are hired to teach!" To most people unfamiliar with academia, this seems so obvious and commonsensical that they might wonder why it had to be said at all, much less emphasized.

In reality, however, it was a revolutionary statement about an unusual college. At most colleges, the faculty do not regard themselves as mere employees but as the movers and shakers of academe—as they are, more's the pity.

If any college were foolish enough to make me president and I were foolish enough to accept, my first order of business would be to see that professors no longer control decisions outside their field of expertise. My second order of business would be to end tenure.

So-called "faculty self-governance" is the ultimate in unaccountable decision-making. No matter how disastrously some policy voted in by the faculty turns out to be, not a single professor can be fired for having voted for it, or even for having led the campaign for that policy.

In what other system of governance—whether in churches or in corporations, in Washington or the state capitols—can people keep on making disastrous decisions without being subject to being removed from their jobs? Even presidents can be impeached and kings forced to abdicate, but tenured professors can vote for all the nonsense they want without the slightest dangers to their jobs.

It is a formula that virtually guarantees irresponsible self-indulgence.

There was a time when college presidents were hired to run the institution, not just raise money for it and serve as its public-relations front man. Names like Nicholas Murray Butler at Columbia and Robert Hutchins at the University of Chicago conjure up a whole era when a college president could shape an institution to his vision of what education was all about.

More important, the president could be fired if it didn't work. Today, when administrators can blame the faculty for most of the key decisions, it is hard to hold anybody accountable.

One of the reasons why even pricey and prestigious universities have many of their undergraduate courses taught by graduate students rather than professors is that professors prefer it that way. It gives the professors more time to hustle research grants and turn out esoteric papers, rather than be bothered teaching elementary stuff that bores them.

My solution for bored professors would be to get rid of them and replace them by people who want to teach. But don't look for my name to be listed as the president of some college any time soon. They say that you should never say "never" but this is one of the few times when you can say it very safely.

LIFE IS CULTURALLY BIASED

THE VITRIOLIC CONTROVERSY DEVELOPING around *The Bell Curve* by Richard Herrnstein and Charles Murray has raised again questions about mental tests and their meaning.

One of the charges made is that the tests are themselves unfair. But, long before the present controversy, someone replied to similar charges by pointing out: "The tests are not unfair. Life is unfair—and tests measure the results."

The same could be said of the charge that tests are "culturally biased." *Life* is culturally biased. We live twice as long as people in some of the poorer parts of the world, not because we are more deserving, individually smarter or otherwise more meritorious, but simply because we had the dumb luck to be born into a culture which produces cures and preventions for deadly diseases that have ravaged the human race for centuries.

The cultural features which advance medical science have by no means been universal. Indeed, they have been fairly recent, as history is measured, even in the civilizations where they now exist. Any test which tests for those kinds of features must be culturally biased—indeed, *should* be culturally biased.

There may well have been individuals born into ignorant and primitive backwaters of the world who had brain cells fully as well-functioning as those of Pasteur, Salk or other medical pioneers, but who never developed the same capabilities and never left a trace of their existence to benefit the rest of mankind. If tested by our culturally biased tests, those individuals would undoubtedly have scored low—and should have, if our purpose was the practical one of picking people actually able to do the kinds of things that needed doing in medical science.

What would have happened under other cultural circumstances is a cosmic question—a question for God, perhaps, but not for intellectuals who act as if they are God.

As limited human beings, we must make our choices among the alternatives actually available. A culture-free society has never been one of those alternatives.

Any test designed to predict future performances in any field or in any society is trying to predict what will happen in a given cultural context. There is nothing inherently sinister about this. These are the conditions we face—or should face.

Few things are discussed as unintelligently as intelligence. Seldom do those who talk—or shout—about this subject bother to define their terms. Is "intelligence" the abstract potentiality that exists at the moment of conception? The developed capabilities with which the same individual faces the world two decades later?

In between, all sorts of things have happened—and happened differently for different individuals and groups. An alcoholic or drug-addicted mother begins damaging her child even before birth. Her irresponsibility, brutality or stupidity is almost certain to do more damage to the child in the years that follow.

What good would it do us to know that child's innate potential at the moment of conception? It certainly would not enable us to predict what it likely to happen now that he is what he is.

Suppose that we had such a miraculous test and discovered that we started out with an Einstein and ended up with an idiot. Would that mean that the test was unfair because it showed that he was an idiot? Or would it mean that life itself was tragically unfair—not only to him, but to the whole society that now has to contend with him as he is?

Maybe such a test would have some social value as a means of shocking us into a realization of what enormities result from subsidizing teenage pregnancy, for example. Yes, it would be hard on all concerned, including the public, to deny welfare to the teenager. But would it be worse than what happens because we cannot bring ourselves to deny it?

Such questions could at least be asked if we had the kind of miraculous test hoped for by some. But there is no sign that we are even close to developing such a test.

The much-vexed question of heredity versus environment, and of possible intergroup differences in inherited potential, are better able to produce heated controversies than enlightened reasoning. Does anyone seriously doubt that heredity plays some role in some differences? Or that it is seldom the whole story?

The Bell Curve itself says: "It should be no surprise to see (as one does every day) blacks functioning at high levels in every intellectually challenging field." But that did not stop the shouts of those who are in the business of shouting. Anyone who actually reads the book—which may not include all of its critics—will discover that race is not even considered in the first 12 chapters. That is hardly what the book is about, though that is what the noise is about.

My own view as a former teacher is that most American students, of whatever background, are operating so far below their capacity that the limits of that capacity is an academic question.

GIVE MONEY AND SHUT UP!

A PICTURE IS SUPPOSED TO BE WORTH a thousand words and a drawing in a recent issue of *The Chronicle of Higher Education* certainly fills that bill. It shows an academic in cap and gown facing a donor holding a bag of money. The academic has his left hand on the bag and his right hand covering the donor's mouth. In other words, give us the money but shut up.

As alumni around the country have become alarmed by the prostitution of college education to ideological indoctrination, and by the totalitarian mindset behind "speech codes" and the kangaroo courts to which they have led, many have tried to influence their alma maters in the direction of traditional education. This has been depicted by academics and by their friends in the media as interferences with academic freedom.

If ever the distinction between freedom and license was crucial, it is on American college campuses today. Courses ostensibly set up to teach freshman writing are routinely turned into courses featuring leftist crusades du jour. Freshman orientation is treated as an opportunity to have spokesmen for homosexual, radical feminist, environmentalist and other causes get a shot at a captive audience.

Conversely, views to the contrary are not only screened out but shouted down, whether originating on campus or in lectures by outside speakers. Blatantly political questions get asked in academic job interviews and those whose answers are out of step find themselves out of luck.

This is not academic freedom. This is a breech of faith.

Unfortunately, the very concept of a breech of faith is foreign to the thinking in academia today. When Yale University was offered $20 million to set up a program in Western Civilization, it not only dragged its feet but instead set up a committee to see how that money could be used to finance yet another countercultural program. When the donor asked for his money back, it was widely depicted as an interference with academic freedom.

The question is not why alumni, both individually and in organizations such as the National Alumni Forum, are trying to restore some integrity to colleges. The question is why it took them so long to act and why so many other donors continue to hand over millions of dollars to institutions and programs antithetical to everything the donors believe in.

Part of the answer is that many donors, alumni, and even trustees have no idea how deep the dry rot goes. Smooth academic administrators know how to talk out of one side of their mouths to the outside world and out of the other to the campus crowd. Another important reason why so much goes unsuspected is that many Americans who love their country, including alumni and donors, simply have no conception of the scope and depth of the hatred of this country and its values by large numbers of academics.

Another fundamental reason for not understanding what is going on is that those who live in the world of bottom-line performance may find it especially difficult to grasp the wholly different world of the intelligentsia. In that world, the only bottom line is what those around you think.

For example, scholars specializing in Africa made many predictions back in the 1960s about the future of the various African nations gaining independence then. Not only were most of these predictions off by miles, a scholar named Peter Duignan, whose predictions stood up much better than most, has never even been hired as a professor at any academic institution.

Being right doesn't count. Saying what others accept is what counts.

If this same standard existed in business, Edsels might today be dominating the automobile industry, while Cadillacs and Lexuses became extinct. But cars have to satisfy others, not just committees inside the automobile industry.

In academia, the committees inside have the last word. Often that word is ideological rather than intellectual. Peter Duignan's writings may be praised in scholarly journals around the world, but those who have been wrong about Africa for 30 years sit on hiring committees judging those who have been right.

Nor is this an isolated case. Anyone who has read or seen Shelby Steele knows what an impressive man he is and how articulate he is. But he has never received a single job offer from an Ivy League college. His opposition to affirmative action alone is enough to put him off limits.

The academic world is not a system that corrects itself. So long as donors continue to conform to academia's desire that they write checks and keep quiet, the dry rot will just spread further and penetrate deeper.

THE "RELIGIOUS RIGHT"

THE "RELIGIOUS RIGHT" SEEMS TO BE the latest preoccupation of the media. Among other things, liberals in the media and in politics have been raising the alarm that the "religious right" is taking over the public schools. Yet, if you look at all the countercultural notions being promoted in the public schools, you will find very little that could be called either religious or conservative.

The values being taught in many public schools today are much more like those you see on Oprah and Donahue than anything you are likely to see on Pat Robertson's program.

Shameless distortions of the truth have become so common in the cultural wars of our time that no one should be surprised that politically active religious groups are being targeted.

A few years ago, a lawsuit was won by a group of parents in Tennessee who objected to the steady diet of anti-religious readings their children were being fed in school. Immediately, liberals declared that these parents were "trying to force their views on others," when in fact they asked only that their own children be exempted from the anti-religious brainwashing. Even a couple of conservative columnists were gullible enough to fall for this complete distortion, though the judge in the case pointed out that the parents had never asked that the anti-religious material be removed from the school.

The idea that it is somehow illegitimate for American citizens to seek redress from their government when they are religious is part of long-standing misunderstanding of the First Amendment. You might as well say that it is unconstitutional for the fire department to put out a fire in a church or for the post office to deliver mail there.

When the First Amendment forbad Congress to create "an establishment of religion," everyone knew what those words meant because the people who wrote the constitution had lived under an established church, the Church of England. Not only was the Church of England supported by taxpayers, including taxpayers who belonged to other churches or to no churches, its members had legal privileges denied to others.

This is what the writers of the constitution forbad Congress to create. For more than a century and a half, no one ever thought that this meant that it was illegal to have prayers in schools or to have nativity scenes on public property at Christmas time. These were just some of the many runaway "interpretations" of the constitution by the headstrong Supreme Courts of our era.

The question is not whether prayer in school was a good idea as public policy. The question is whether it was forbidden by the constitution or whether the learned justices lied through their teeth when they said that it was.

They lied. But the political question today is not whether the Supreme Court overstepped its bounds, as it did, but whether those whose legitimate role is policy-making should now make prayer in school a public policy. If the Supreme Court wants to salvage its honor and its credibility by reversing the prayer-in-school decision, that would be fine, though unlikely.

Politicians creating prayers for the public schools cannot be something that many religious or non-religious people really want to see. Bland, one-size-fits-all prayers should be as offensive to religious people as the idea of pressuring children from non-religious homes to take part hypocritically would be to others.

If religious conservatives simply react to the Supreme Court's mistakes or dishonesty by trying to force a prayer-in-school policy as a matter of political muscle-flexing, they will miss a golden opportunity to fight the values battles that need to be fought with allies who would be with them on other issues, but not on this one.

At a time when public schools across the country are systematically pushing countercultural ideas and ridiculing traditional values, instead of teaching the academic subjects they are paid to teach, the strongest and broadest opposition needs to be mounted against such brainwashing. Not only Christians of all sorts but Jews, Moslems and agnostics need to be enlisted in this battle.

The counterculture is already solidly entrenched in the public schools and dislodging them will take all the allies and efforts that can be mustered. A measure of the political seriousness of religious conservatives will be whether they want to make this general fight for traditional values their priority and win, or go down to defeat with the banner of prayer-in-school nailed to their masthead.

BLACK HISTORY LESSON

AN OLD BUDDY OF MINE USED to say, "Don't do me no favors, break my neck!"

That remark might apply to much of the recent history of black Americans. In many ways, blacks were more successful in overcoming the opposition of racists than in overcoming the effects of those who thought they were helping.

The centerpiece of the civil rights struggle was the Supreme Court's landmark decision in 1954 outlawing racial segregation in the case of Brown vs. Board of Education. Racially segregated and grossly unequal schooling was long overdue to be struck down, but the pattern of thinking set in motion by the Brown case has led into many blind alleys.

Racial integration and government help became the watchwords of a whole generation of minority leaders and white liberals. Where has it led?

Is the education of black youngsters better today than it was before the great social, judicial and political crusades to mix and match students by race through busing and other schemes?

Perhaps in some places it is, but in the great urban ghettoes that education is much inferior to what it was when I was going to school in Harlem back in the 1940s. Relying on records, rather than nostalgia, let us look at how the school I went to—P.S.5, Manhattan— stacked up against white working class schools on the lower east side of New York at the same time.

In neither neighborhood did the schools match the performances of schools in affluent neighborhoods, where parents were better educated. But neither were they miles behind, like today. Whether in Harlem or on the lower east side, students were grouped by ability and the best classes offered an education that would allow their students to go anywhere and compete with anybody.

As of December 1941, test scores for Harlem students in the second semester of the 6th grade were 5.2 in understanding both paragraph meaning and word meaning, while in lower east side schools like P.S. 23 and P.S. 130 these scores were 5.1 in paragraph meaning and 4.5 and 4.7, respectively, in word meaning.

The city-wide average was 6.8, so these kids were behind, but not out of it completely—and youngsters in the high ability classes in both places had what it took to go on to become educated, middle class adults.

In tests given in May 1947, Harlem students in the third grade at P.S.5 matched the city-wide average in understanding both paragraph meaning and word meaning, and exceeded the city-wide average in arithmetic. Lower east side students in P.S. 23 and P.S.130 were just slightly below the city-wide average at that point. In other years, the lower east side youngsters had the edge on the Harlem students—but it was only an edge either way.

Compare that with today, when it is taken for granted that ghetto schools will perform miles behind everyone else—and when everyone from the National Education Association to the N.A.A.C.P. has "politically correct" explanations for these failures, instead of facing the fact that performances were once so much better, without any of the liberal "prerequisites" they are peddling today.

Once, when my niece was down on herself for not having made better use of her opportunities, she said, "I went to the same school you went to, Uncle Tommy."

"No," I told her, "you went to the same *building* I went to—but by the time you got there, it was no longer the same school."

Education is just one of the big casualties of the social theories and social engineering of the past generation. The continual undermining of law and order, by people who considered the very phrase itself as racist, has damaged the black community worse than any other.

Is anyone aware that the murder rate among blacks was declining sharply for years before the new theories of crime began to be applied in the 1960s and new criminals' "rights" were created out of thin air by liberal Supreme Court justices? After that, the murder rates sky-rocketed for everyone, along with crime rates in general.

This history has not only been ignored, it has been erased and political fantasies recorded over it. To admit that Harlem was a lot safer during the 1930s and 1940s than it is today would be to expose the hollowness of the "politically correct" theory that poverty and discrimination cause crime. My generation had far more poverty and discrimination and far less crime.

Perhaps the most dangerous "favor" done to blacks has been the making of excuses for all their problems. All human beings are so imperfect, no matter what color wrapping they come in, that to exempt any group from the standards of performance and behavior expected of others is not a blessing but a curse.

Many white liberals have adopted blacks as mascots, in order to "make a statement" against American society. But mascots are only symbols, and their well-being is seldom a top priority.

While those liberals who have adopted blacks as mascots, and those black "leaders" who go along to get along, may be able to point to all sorts of political benefits they have delivered, that is not enough to offset ruining education, law and order, and the family. Nothing could be.

TOO MUCH MONEY IN ACADEME?

"SEND MONEY" HAS LONG BEEN the traditional theme of college students' letters to their parents. For more than a quarter of a century, that has also been the central theme of the colleges' own messages to the public, to the state legislatures and to the federal government.

Now a college president is saying that vast amounts of government money have been the main cause of the distortion and degeneration of undergraduate education in America. He is Dr. George Roche, president of Hillsdale College, which accepts no government money. Hillsdale also does not go along with many of the trendy and often disastrous experiments taking place at other colleges.

Hillsdale does not allow male and female students to spend the night in each other's rooms, and does not even have condom-dispensing machines. That's how out of step it is.

In his new book, *The Fall of the Ivory Tower,* Dr. Roche says that it is the other colleges which have gotten out of step with the traditional values of this country and which have allowed educational standards to fall. His indictment is very specific and very extensive—and very true.

The biggest casualty of government largesse to colleges and universities has been undergraduate teaching. Billions of dollars of federal research grants have taken professors out of the classroom on campuses across the country and replaced them with graduate students only a few years older than the undergraduates they are teaching.

These graduate students, usually called "teaching assistants," do not just assist professors with grading or laboratory sessions. They teach courses themselves—half of all freshmen courses at the University of North Carolina, half of all undergraduate courses at Princeton, and nearly half of all undergraduate mathematics courses nationwide.

George Roche calls it "bait-and-switch" advertising when colleges send out pretty brochures boasting of the wonderful professors they have and then present the entering freshmen with unknown graduate students as their teachers.

Why are the colleges doing this? Because huge government research grants make star professors too valuable to waste on anything so inconsequential as teaching students. A number of universities have government grants adding up to hundreds of millions of dollars for each university and Johns Hopkins has research grants topping half a billion.

Students' tuition cannot compete with that kind of money for the time and attention of top professors. Moreover, it is not just research money for studies in medicine, science or engineering. The federal treasury is thrown wide open to finance research and writing on everything from the sublime to the ridiculous.

Grants from the National Endowment for the Humanities have financed studies on the harp tradition in Uganda, raccoon hunting and hand fishing, and the World War II fictitious character, "Rosie the riveter." The "scholarly" papers presented at the annual meetings of the Modern Language Association have much less to do with language than with far-out sex and off-the-wall theories of literature. Much of this shows your tax dollars at work.

As an insider in academia, Dr. Roche knows all the tricks by which government money is gotten, even though his college refuses to take any. He also knows the accounting tricks by which colleges can present "deficits" or "surpluses" according to whichever is politically expedient at the moment—and regardless of the actual financial condition of the institution.

He details the corruption of even legitimate scientific and medical research and the frauds which have been uncovered in recent years. These frauds are promoted by the pressures to come up with something "exciting" to keep the big bucks rolling in. Medical fraud is particularly dangerous because the misinformation it produces can prove to be damaging or even fatal to patients.

Given the enormous importance of large government grants, university officials have often been far less concerned about fraudulent research than about those who expose it. The Harvard medical school, the University of Pittsburgh and Rockefeller University are just some of the places where the administration took a protective approach toward those who perpetuated fraud and a hostile approach to those who reported it.

The Fall of the Ivory Tower details many ways in which colleges and universities have sold their souls and betrayed their trust in pursuit of big money. To George Roche, the present financial hard times hitting many academic institutions are among the few hopeful signs for the future, though he says colleges and universities "still have an awful lot of money to squander."

Dr. Roche also foresees "a popular backlash against colleges and universities for years to come"—and sees that as another factor forcing them to clean up their act. In this context, the biggest danger is that the alumni, the state legislatures and the federal government will turn soft and bail out academia once again.

Shameless deception has become increasingly pervasive in pursuit of government money—only one sign of the moral bankruptcy of much of American higher education. The corruption surrounding college athletics is so pervasive that the new scandals which are constantly being uncovered are barely considered news and no one is really shocked any more. Double standards for minority students are officially denied on most campuses, but it is an open secret on these same campuses that such double standards apply not only in admissions but even in grading and in standards of behavior.

EDUCATION FOLLIES

IN A WORLD WHERE SCHOOLS seem desperate to find things to do to avoid teaching academic subjects, San Francisco's Lowell High School still teaches the traditional subjects—and teaches them well enough to be nationally recognized as an outstanding school.

Like other schools that teach real subjects—instead of tree-hugging and psycho-babble—Lowell H. S. has a waiting list of students who want to get in.

In a competitive economy, this would lead other schools to try to become more like Lowell, even if that meant giving up social crusades, innumerable fads that are dignified with the word "innovation," and miscellaneous cute fluff. But, since public schools are a monopoly, they continue to ignore what the parents, students, and taxpayers want, and continue to do whatever is fashionable with the National Education Association.

As for the big backlog of applicants to Lowell High School, the education bureaucracy rations admissions by racial quotas. There is competition by grades and test scores—but only against students from your own racial or ethnic category.

Obviously, the more academically capable your group is, the harder it is to get into Lowell High School. If you are a Chinese American student, you have to make a score of 66 points out of a perfect 69 to get in. But if you are white, then 59 is good enough, and if you are black or Hispanic, 54 is good enough.

Is this America? Or are we trying to become like the Balkans?

Group quotas have virtually a money-back guarantee that they will create polarization and inflame hostility. They have done this in India, where intergroup riots regularly kill several times as many people as died in last year's Los Angeles riots. Quotas and polarization go together from Fiji in the South Pacific to Malaysia and Sri Lanka in Asia, Nigeria and other countries in Africa, and of course Lebanon in the Middle East.

Saint Paul had a great revelation and conversion on the road to Damascus. Will our quota-mongers ever have a revelation and conversion before we go further on the road to Beirut?

Not very likely. There is no pressure on them to adjust to reality. With a government monopoly ensuring them a supply of customers, with iron-clad tenure protecting their jobs, and with seniority rather than performance determining their salaries, why should the education establishment worry about anything as irrelevant as reality?

The San Francisco school system is by no means unique in being free to do pretty much what they feel like, regardless of the consequences to other people's education. Self-indulgence in whatever fads catch their fancy is a result that should not be surprising.

What is surprising is how quietly the parents and taxpayers accept all this. Now and then there are outcries when parents discover how raw the "sex education" given to young children is. But the more fundamental question is: Where does anyone get the nerve to preempt the parents' decision as to when and how their own children should be introduced to sex?

Perhaps even more to the point, where do these so-called "educators"—who have failed miserably to educate—get the nerve to play social engineers and psychological manipulators with other people's children?

By virtually every test ever administered over the past several decades, people coming out of schools of education are the dregs of the college population. Yet somehow they have managed to intimidate parents into believing that teachers and school administrators have some mysterious "expertise" about education which no one should dare to question.

Among the many fatuous ideas which find a home in the empty heads of "educators" is the notion that student performances should not be graded. Elementary schools in Los Angeles have stopped giving failing grades, and recently elementary schools in the city of Alameda stopped giving grades at all.

In San Jose, grades have been replaced by words like "independent," "confident," "capable," "developing," "limited," and "emergent." Figuring out what any of this means is like reading tea leaves. When they say that your kid is "emergent" that means, according to the official manual, that he "does not have ability to read print independently."

Mush and money are the main preoccupations of American schools. Despite innumerable studies showing virtually no correlation between the money spent on education and the amount learned, the "educators" insist that all our problems are due to "inadequate funding."

Their trump card is to say that the resistance of affluent parents to equalizing expenditures in all school districts proves that expenditures do matter. In reality, all that it proves is that nobody gives up anything willingly.

Palo Alto High School, located across the street from Stanford University, has seven tennis courts, a swimming pool, a huge campus and spacious, tree-shaded parking lots. The fact that they want to hang onto this lifestyle in no way proves anything about education.

The main benefit from equalizing expenditures in all schools would be that this red herring would no longer be able to distract us from the many and severe problems of American education.

But, before any meaningful improvement can take place, we have got to stop taking guff from these shallow people and stop taking excuses.

THE SCHOOL OF HARD KNOCKS

SOME OF THE MOST SHALLOW AND ILLOGICAL letters I receive are from school teachers, so I was a little less surprised than some others by an episode at Canarsie High School in New York.

In one of the innumerable "activities" which substitute for education in American public schools, Canarsie High decided to jump on the "multicultural" bandwagon and have an International Cultural Fair, where students could present the culturally distinctive features of their own racial or ethnic group.

The local newspaper, the *Canarsie Courier.* had a couple of people covering the event. One wrote an essay expressing his shock at seeing "litter-strewn hallways, the students playing handball in the halls in disregard of passers-by, and the obscenities from both male and female students, as well as from the security guards. He suggested that someone should "take a Singapore switch to the backsides of some of these kids."

The response to this essay was as in-your-face as the behavior he had criticized. A teacher at Canarsie wrote to the newspaper that its writer's remarks were a "tirade" while the students' behavior was downgraded to "questionable." Without denying the truth of what was reported, its "negativism" was called "a grave injustice to the students and teachers at Canarsie High School."

Then came the letters from the students—or perhaps pupils might be a more accurate term, since there was little evidence from their letters that they had studied anything. The first letter began: "Last week in Canarsie High when had the International Cultural Fair and you get the name worng."

No, that's not my typo or my grammar. That's what he wrote.

Another "student" said that she was shocked that "an Editor (you call yourself) whom doesn't go to Canarsie High School and dosen't participate in our activies would write such lies." Moreover, she said: "Were kids what more do you want."

If what was said was a lie, how could she make an excuse for something that didn't happen? Logic, however, is one of those old-fashioned things that play very little role in today's education.

Another "student" expressed his disappointment this way: "Always thought Canarsie Courier alway tell truth, justice and eventruly I was wrong."

Yet another "student" wrote: "Maybe you think high school is a monastarey or a convent, but suprise its not." She added: "The teachers are well groomed and up to parr. They reach above and beyond the standards of any NYC High School and I am very greatful to have such quality people taking the time out to give a hoot."

Seldom is there an occasion to criticize anyone for excessive gratitude but this is one of those occasions. On the other hand, I am certainly "greatful" that I never went to a school like Canarsie High.

Another pupil wrote in to defend the security guards because "the do their jobs every good, and if someone don't have a pass or/and an I.d card, you are not getting passed them." He suggested that if the editor had forgotten what it was like being a kid, he should "go back to the passed."

Still another pupil complained that the editor "totaly forgot" to write about the fair that he came to cover.

Finally, one pupil seized upon the editor's mention of having to dodge a tennis ball while walking through the hall. "You must of been very scared of that tennis ball to dodge it," he said. Then he closed with the pop psychology so fashionable in educational circles: "You really hated this school when you where young didn't you?"

It gets worse. An adult wrote in to castigate the newspaper for printing the pupils' letters with all their mistakes. He asked:

"What did you achieve by showing the deficiencies of these fine youngsters who feel good about their school and what it's offering them. At a time when school morale is low, and drop outs are at a high what was the point?"

All this is vintage response to criticisms of the collapse of education in American public schools. Psychoanalyze the critics, accuse them of negativism, challenge their honesty even if you cannot challenge their facts. In short, do anything to avoid confronting the truth.

The Canarsie "students" are all too typical in having lots of opinions and lots of brass—and having no conception of logic or evidence. Where would they get such analytical skills? Certainly not from the typical teacher of today.

All is not lost. There were a few signs of sanity in this episode. A couple of adults wrote in to express shock at the high school pupils' obvious ignorance. One said, "they could all spend a lot less time in Multi-Cultural activities and a lot more time in learning grammar and spelling." A grandmother wrote that when her grandchildren are ready to go to high school, "I will clean public toilets to be able to send them to a parochial high school."

EDUCATION ON TAPE?

I WAS SKEPTICAL WHEN A VERY knowledgeable university president told me that videotaped college lectures were a coming thing and had a potential for major impact on American higher education. But three academic institutions in North Dakota have already set up a televised lecture system serving students on all three campuses simultaneously.

In this sophisticated system, students located hundreds of miles away can engage in televised discussions with professors and their distant classmates. Moreover, they not only are able to take individual courses this way, they can earn a college degree in business administration, education or nursing solely through televised courses.

In these tight financial times, when state colleges and universities are finding it harder than ever to make ends meet and state legislators are reluctant to ask taxpayers to carry a much heavier load, the pressures toward cost-saving methods of teaching are likely to be great. It is probably no accident that the three institutions which have set up this joint television network are all state schools: The University of North Dakota, North Dakota State University and North Dakota State College of Science.

No doubt it will be a long time before Ivy League colleges allow televised education to replace traditional methods of teaching. For one thing, if parents could see televised lectures from Ivy League colleges and compare them with televised lectures from lesser-known institutions, they might decide that they cannot see any difference sufficient to justify straining the family budget to come up with the huge tuitions charged at big-name colleges.

In more than a few cases, Ivy League lectures would not be as good as lectures on the same subjects at many liberal arts colleges which specialize in teaching, rather than in turning out research. A lot of people in big-name institutions stand to lose big if televised college courses become widespread.

A lot of other people stand to benefit, however. People who cannot afford the heavy expense of going away to live on a college campus can get an education via the television screen where they live. It will not be the same—but sometimes it will be better.

The costly adolescent manias of the campus, from fraternities to football and from political crusades to the drug culture, are not additions to education but distractions from it. The televised lectures themselves may be better in many cases because professors can be watched not only by their students but also by academic administrators, trustees, the public and both state and federal officials.

"You have to do your homework," a North Dakota professor says of televised teaching. "You can't just walk in and wing it."

All too many professors not only wing it but dog it, even in places that charge top-dollar tuition. The faculty at many institutions know that their future does not depend on how good they are at teaching but on how much research they publish and how much money they bring on campus in research grants.

Televised lectures would allow much better quality control, not only as regards teaching technique but also as regards monitoring the quality of the professor's own knowledge and analytical ability. Videotapes of a professor's lectures could be evaluated by leading scholars in his field, whether those scholars were on the same campus or thousands of miles away at another academic institution or think tank.

Although the televised lecture system in North Dakota broadcasts live, there is no reason why videotapes would not be good in some subjects—especially as replacement for professors who currently lecture to classes with hundreds of students each, sometimes even exceeding a thousand. Typically, there is no live interaction with such a huge audience, so there is nothing to lose by watching a videotape instead.

Videotapes will never replace the small class discussing their work with their instructor around a seminar table. But students at most state universities get very little of that kind of personalized education now.

Professors who lecture from the same yellowed notes for years on end might just as well be replaced by one videotaped lecture that can be played as long as the department has found no significant development in that field which is missing.

Then there are the visiting professors who may be top scholars in their specialties. A small liberal arts college which could hardly afford to pay the salaries of academic superstars every year may nevertheless be able to afford one or two a year as visiting professors and preserve their lectures on tape for use in later years.

Imagine Podunk A & M being able to teach its students economics with videotapes of lectures by Milton Friedman, law with videotapes of Robert Bork's lectures and political science with lectures by Henry Kissinger. Many heavyweight scholars who find the repressive atmosphere of "political correctness" on campus to be more than they feel like putting up with could nevertheless share their knowledge and insights with students via the television screen.

Years from now, someone may look back and discover that a real revolution began quietly in North Dakota in 1994.

SUCCESSFUL SCHOOLS AND FAILING POLITICS

IN THE JUNE 2, 1997 ISSUE of *Forbes* magazine, historian Diane Ravitch offers a heart-warming contemporary story about a ghetto school in Brooklyn where the children are doing far better academically than in most ghetto schools—or a lot of non-ghetto schools, for that matter.

The school is P.S. 161 in the poor Crown Heights section of Brooklyn. Professor Ravitch found that four-fifths of the third-graders there met the state reading standards for their grade. In fact, more than one-third of these third-graders met the state reading standards for the sixth grade.

With so many people across the country wringing their hands over the poor quality of education for black children, you might think that there would be great cheering over such results and that the principal would be regarded as a national hero. But I doubt that this will happen.

Twenty years ago, I wrote about similar black schools in various parts of the country and found that the best I could hope for was indifference. Where there was any reaction, it was usually hostility, since successful black schools seemed to undermine the crusade for racial mixing and matching of students, as well as the crusades for more federal money.

Professor Ravitch points out that the politicians in Washington already know that the billions of dollars they are pouring down a bottomless pit in the name of educating ghetto children are accomplishing nothing—at least nothing beneficial to those children. But this money is enormously beneficial to the politicians.

First of all, it makes a big public show of their "commitment" and makes their political opponents vulnerable to the charge that they lack "compassion" when these opponents are unwilling to spend as freely on the many failed programs. More than that, free spending gains the political support of local "community leaders" who are able to build their own little empires with the taxpayers' money, hiring their friends, relatives and political allies to work on the programs created.

In many poor communities, as in many Third World countries, the readiest source of wealth is the public treasury. Desperate struggles to gain access to political office and the money this represents, as well as high levels of corruption, are the predictable results in both cases.

Teachers' unions also have their agendas that require more money from taxpayers. These unions need victories, in order to maintain membership support. These victories have to be things that can be measured in higher pay, smaller class sizes and other tangible benefits to their members—whether or not these things make the slightest difference to the school children.

At P.S. 161 in Brooklyn, for example, class sizes range up to 35 children per class. In some of the high-quality black schools I studied 20 years ago, class sizes were even larger.

But smaller class size is a political symbol, as well as a means of creating more jobs for teachers, so it is promoted to the public as a sacred goal and to the union's membership as a trophy of victory.

If all this cynical politicking over education did nothing worse than waste some more money, it would hardly be worth getting upset about. But, for many of the poorest children, education is their one ticket out of poverty. If they miss that train, they miss everything: They are history before they are teenagers.

Who is to fight the battles for these children's interests? The Congressional Black Caucus is virtually a wholly-owned subsidary of the largest teachers' union, the National Education Association, which shells out millions of dollars a year to the Democrats.

The only people who can be relied on to put these children's interests first are their own parents. Yet these parents are often too poor to be able to pull their children out of rotten public schools and put them elsewhere. Various kinds of parental choice policies, whether based on vouchers or some other method, would allow the well-being of these children to become important.

Needless to say, the Congressional Black Caucus is bitterly opposed to vouchers and anything else that would offend their sponsors, the National Education Association.

In the meantime, we have P.S. 161 in Brooklyn as an example of what can be accomplished with children who are just as poor and just as black as other kids who are failing miserably in other schools all across the country.

PART VII
RANDOM THOUGHTS

RANDOM THOUGHTS

RANDOM THOUGHTS ON THE PASSING SCENE:

If truth-in-labeling laws applied to panhandlers, then a lot of guys who carry signs saying "hungry" would have to change that to "thirsty."

The one thing that no policy will ever change is the past.

People who are trying to prove something usually don't prove anything, except what jerks they are.

Politics is the art of finding clever reasons for doing dumb things.

For years after the end of World War II, there were rumors that Hitler was still alive and in hiding somewhere. If so, now is the time for him to come on out. He can say "mistakes were made," express remorse and do his 200 hours of community service. Then he can sell his story to Oliver Stone to make a movie showing how the war was all the fault of Churchill and Roosevelt.

Liberals have never understood the significance of that great line from *On the Waterfront,* where Marlon Brando says: "I coulda been a contender!" Nothing you can give anybody is a substitute for letting him achieve on his own.

You can't stop people from saying bad things about you. All you can do is make them liars.

People who think that they are too good for their jobs are usually not good enough.

The problems growing out of short cuts and abbreviations have probably wasted far more time than these short cuts and abbreviations will ever save.

Some people say that I am overweight. But, after looking at the height and weight charts, I prefer to say that I am six inches too short.

There is no greater indictment of judges than the fact that honest men are afraid to go into court, while criminals swagger out through its revolving doors.

Many people need more help than they deserve. That's why there are families.

We pay our public officials too much for what they are and too little for what we want them to be.

When you want to help people, you tell them the truth. When you want to help yourself, you tell them what they want to hear.

The public can get the bums off the streets faster than all the policemen in the country, just by not giving them money. Everybody doesn't have to stop, just enough to make the racket no longer worth it.

It always amazes me how many people there are who never seem to understand that what they have done has contributed to the consequences that followed.

California students in Monroe High School and Cleveland High School were surprised to learn that their schools were named for presidents. One girl at Cleveland H.S. said: "I thought it was named for that city in Canada."

It is painful to watch how inconsiderate so many people are of the slow-moving elderly. People out walking with them all but pull them along, even when it is obvious that they cannot go any faster. What is the point of pressuring or embarrassing someone like that?

We are among the biggest fools in history if we keep on paying people to make us hate each other. Whether it is called by pretty names like "multiculturalism," "diversity" or "gender awareness," that is what it all boils down to.

"Funding" is one of the big phony words of our times—used by people too squeamish to say "money" but not too proud to take it, usually from the taxpayers.

It has been said that armed civilians kill more criminals than the police do. If so, that is the strongest argument against gun control. At least those particular criminals will never walk the streets again, as they are likely to do if they go into the revolving door of our legal system.

Most of the Democrats who have run for President in the past 25 years—and all who have run successfully—have camouflaged their liberalism. Yet exposing the fraud leads to media charges of "negative" campaigning.

It is not necessarily a bad thing for young people to become disillusioned with their idols, if their own development has reached the point where they no longer need idols. Disillusionment is an inoculation against future gullibility.

It is hard to trust very good-looking women. You just know that they have been getting away with murder all their lives.

One of the miracles of faith is the liberals' belief that criminals will stop being armed if we ban guns. We have already banned crime and that doesn't stop them from committing it.

A quote to remember: "You know, doing what is right is easy. The problem is knowing what is right." Lyndon Johnson said that—and much of his legislation painfully illustrated the difference between good intentions and good results.

I know that many people have no respect at all for Bill Clinton. Still, I was surprised to see an advertisement for toilet paper with his picture printed on each sheet.

Those who want to be "politically correct" must stay on their toes because new terms are being coined all the time. You may know that waiters and waitresses should be referred to as "wait persons" or "servers," but did you know that pets must now be referred to as "animal companions" and prostitutes as "sex workers"?

There must be a hundred people who know what needs to be done for every one who is prepared to do it.

There seem to be many "modern" parents who think that raising children is something you can do in your spare time, letting nursery schools and the like carry the load when the parents are busy with "important" things.

We are living in an era when sanity is controversial and insanity is just another viewpoint—and degeneracy only another lifestyle.

It is important that young children be able to rely on their parents completely—and equally important that grown children not be able to.

Have you ever seen some painting, writing, or clothing that you thought looked awful? Some music that you thought sounded terrible? You are free to say so only when these are products of Western civilization. Say that about something from some other culture and you are considered a terrible person, if not a racist.

With so many people—young people especially—the problem is not that they cannot figure out complicated things. The problem is that they will not take the trouble to do simple things and to do them right.

Never try to discuss important business with any organization during lunch time, when the regular staff are eating and the substitutes are on duty.

I can understand that some people like to drive slowly. What I cannot understand is why they get in the fast lane to do it.

If the Democrats came up with a plan for all Americans to jump off a thousand-foot cliff tomorrow, some Republicans would come up with an "alternative" plan in which we would all jump off a 500-foot cliff next week.

I was pained when I first read Joseph Schumpeter's statement, "You cannot carry people up the ladder." I have been even more pained over the years finding out the hard way that he was right.

There seem to be growing numbers of people who feel that those who disagree with them are not merely mistaken but malign, not merely in error but in sin.

The grand fallacy of the political left is that evil is localized in some set of "oppressors" from whom we can be "liberated." That is also its great attraction, for it allows people to attribute their dissatisfactions to other people.

If you have trouble visualizing the billions and trillions of dollars that politicians talk about (and spend) in Washington, think of it this way: A billion seconds ago, John F. Kennedy was President of the United States. And a trillion seconds ago no one on this planet could read or write.

The pacifist mindset is truly a triumph of hope over centuries of experience. One lady writes: "I believe attacking someone for attacking you just fosters more attack and more and never resolves anything." Should we have sat still with folded hands while Hitler took over the world? And would either this lady or I still be here to discuss the issue if he had?

The purpose of politics is not to solve problems but to find problems to justify the expansion of government power and an increase in taxes.

Being slick is the way to gain little things and lose big things.

I have never understood why it is "greed" to want to keep the money you have earned but not greed to want to take somebody else's money.

What an irony that Richard Nixon was dying while Hillary Clinton was making her own "Checkers" speech. Even a woman with a reputation for being vicious and foul-mouthed among those who have actually dealt with her can still win over a large part of the media by coming on as Little Girl Nice. Anita Hill proved that in 1991 and Hillary has just proved it again.

After all the media puffing up of retiring Justice Harry Blackmun, the liberal "New Republic" magazine has finally said that the emperor has no clothes, that "the liberal lionization of him is cynical" because it is based on nothing more than his having voted for things they liked. Maybe in another fifty years, we can expect similar candor about other justices who have been puffed up for purely political reasons.

When I give a book to a young person starting out in life, I often include on the fly leaf a quotation from the great economist David Ricardo. He wrote to a friend on December 22, 1818: "I wish that I may never think the smiles of the great and powerful a sufficient inducement to turn aside from the straight path of honesty and the convictions of my own mind."

Those who are for turning criminals loose on all sorts of grounds might ponder the words of Edmund Burke, two centuries ago: "There is no safety for honest men but by believing all possible evil of evil men."

Those who talk about helping "the little people" give me a pain. People are the same size, and have the same importance as human beings, whether they are rich or poor. Paternalism toward others has long been camouflage for power and an ego trip for oneself.

People who have been arguing for years for the brotherhood of man are now surprised to discover that it is true, especially when it means that individuals from minority groups can be just as racist as individuals from the majority.

Search committees looking for college presidents should have a stop watch so that they can tell how long each candidate can talk without using the word "diversity."

I cannot understand people who say that minorities should be represented everywhere and yet are upset when there are blacks represented in the conservative movement.

There is no such thing as uncontaminated air or uncontaminated water—or uncontaminated anything else. The only rational question is how much you are prepared to pay to remove what percentage of the impurities. Zealots of course have no interest in that question. The net result is that the government is spending bundles of money to reduce trivial traces of chemicals.

The first rule of bureaucracy is that the bureaucracy is never wrong. If they say you didn't pay your bill, then you didn't pay it, even if you have the canceled check in your hand.

Are we all going to have to become nudists, in order to get through airport security machines?

Historians of the future will have a hard time figuring out how so many organized groups of strident jackasses succeeded in leading us around by the nose and morally intimidating the majority into silence.

When will airlines learn that their passengers prefer food that tastes good to food that looks fancy and sounds pretentious, but tastes like leather and cardboard?

Some medicine bottle caps are on so tight that, if you are strong enough to get them off, you probably aren't all that sick.

Women may lie about their age to other people, but men lie about their age to themselves. That is why middle-aged men injure themselves in athletic activities intended for younger men.

The ideas of the political left are not bad ideas. They just don't apply to human beings. That is why the left has always had to try to change human nature, whether through "re-education" camps, "brainwashing" in China, creating a "Soviet Man" in the U.S.S.R., or "values clarification" programs in American schools.

The anointed talk about the sexuality of the young as if they had discovered it and copyrighted it. Why do they think people in olden times had such things as chaperones, early marriage, separate dormitories, and a thousand other ways of trying to cope with youthful sexuality and its consequences?

How can you insulate people from reality without having them become unrealistic in their decisions and behavior? Yet many people try to provide such insulation to their own adolescent or adult children, and governments try to provide it to all the various clients of the welfare state.

There is so much money, and so much publicity, available for saying far-out things that we are lucky to hear any common sense at all.

It always amazes me that there are people who go out of their way to be difficult—and who are then surprised and bitter when they are fired, divorced or dropped as friends.

There is something obscene about people holding protest rallies in order to try to keep getting money that someone else worked for.

If you are not prepared to get rid of tenure, then you are not going to change our disastrous educational system in any fundamental way.

Whatever cosmetic "reforms" come and go, the same people will keep on doing the same things as long as they have iron-clad job guarantees.

Of all the children I have known who continued to live with their parents after becoming adults, none has turned out well.

When you realize that Germans were brewing beer back in the days of the Roman Empire, how surprised should you be to discover that most of the leading breweries in the United States—Budweiser, Coors, Miller, etc.—were founded by people of German ancestry? Those who expect ethnic or other groups to be randomly distributed are either ignorant of history or oblivious to cause and effect.

Much of what is called "public service" is make-work for people who have degrees but no skills that would get them the kind of money and importance they feel entitled to in the marketplace.

People who pride themselves on their "complexity" and deride others for being "simplistic" should realize that the truth is often not very complicated. What gets complex is evading the truth.

They say that those who can, do—and those who can't teach. Those who can't teach, indoctrinate.

Some people think that, if they are given certain information in confidence, it is OK to tell someone else in confidence.

A poll shows that the percentage of the public expressing great confidence in our colleges and universities has fallen from 66 percent in 1966 to 25 percent in 1994. The public is right. They do not deserve confidence.

In a letter from a reader: "No one is useless: a person with no good qualities can always serve as a bad example."

Where are all the "privacy" advocates in politics when companies selling everything from newspapers to real estate are making unsolicited phone calls to people's homes—even people with unlisted numbers—waking up babies, disturbing sick people, interrupting lovers, etc.?

The best way to find out what people are really like is to turn your back.

One of the purest of all loves is the love of a bureaucrat for a routine. This is not a love based on crass considerations of efficiency. The routine is loved for its own sweet sake.

Some people who are very dissatisfied with their lives nevertheless have no intention of changing their own behavior. They want to keep on doing what they have always done, but just have it turn out differently.

Beware of anyone who answers your question before you have finished asking it.

The number one rule of traffic safety is: Fools have the right of way. Anyone who qualifies for this privilege should be given it.

Senator Daniel Patrick Moynihan gave a chilling glimpse of how our world has changed, when he said: "In 1943, there were exactly forty-four homicides by gunshot in all of the City of New York. Last year there were 1,499."

One of the most pathetic—and dangerous—signs of our times is the growing number of individuals and groups who believe that no one can possibly disagree with them for any honest reason.

Those who believe that "basic necessities" should belong to people as a matter of right ignore the implication—that people are to work only for amenities, frivolities, and ego. Will that mean more work or less work? And if less, where are all those "basic necessities" coming from that the government is supposed to hand out?

If the government punishes people for being productive by hitting them with big tax increases, and rewards people for being unproductive by giving them entitlements to the taxpayers' money, how is that likely to lead to a more productive economy?

People who believe in conspiracy theories should ask themselves: Have you ever tried to keep a secret among five people? Even Mafia dons get squealed on.

Heterosexuals and homosexuals should both stay in the closet. Who wants to hear about other people's sex lives?

Advice to the young: You don't have to listen to anybody. You can learn everything from your own personal experience. Of course, you will be at least 50 years old by the time you know what you need to know at 25.

One of the many mysteries of human beings is why some people will never pass on the message you leave. They must either abbreviate it, rephrase it, or otherwise change it. The mischief this can create never seems to occur to them.

There are two kinds of people in this world—those who are "going to" do something and those who actually do it.

If it were up to me, the age of adulthood would never have been lowered from 21 to 18. It would have been raised to 30. In recent decades, people have been taking longer and longer to mature—and increasing numbers never make it.

People who are lax about their personal security should realize that burglars and muggers make a living off other people's carelessness.

I never cease to be amazed at the people who want to make your decision for you, instead of supplying you with the information you need to make your own decision.

Many of the dangerous things that drivers do are not likely to save them even 10 seconds. When you bet your life against 10 seconds, that is giving bigger odds than you are ever likely to get in Las Vegas.

Most problems do not get solved. They get superseded by other concerns.

"No justice, no peace" is yet another of the many clever but shallow and irresponsible phrases of our time. No situation in any society of human beings is likely to be regarded as justice by everyone. Does that mean that everlasting violence is justified?

The last thing you want to do is promote tribalism when you are one of the smaller tribes. Yet minority "leaders" do this because it promotes their individual self-interest, regardless of what bad effects this will have on others, including their followers.

How come the yellow pages list movers but not shakers?

The superstitions of intellectuals are still superstitions—and they have a lot of them. The real question is why we keep listening to them, after their nostrums have failed time and time again.

Have theorists wreaked more havoc than war? It is too close to call. Wars may be more destructive while they are raging, but they occur only at intervals, while half-baked theories are constantly creating needless disasters.

Signs of our times: Lawrence University and a five-college group including Amherst, Smith, Mount Holyoke, Hampshire and the University of Massachusetts advertised jobs for teaching fellows by race in the September 7th issue of *The Chronicle of Higher Education.* Whites need not apply.

When will television sports programs learn that sports fans want to see the action on the field—not psychobabble by either announcers or athletes? And when will the camera men learn that people want to see what is happening—not what cute angles they can think up?

Someone has suggested that most so-called "grassroots" political movements should be called Astroturf movements instead, since they are usually artificially created.

One of the depressing things about reading ancient history is that it makes you realize how long human beings have been the way they are—and how unlikely they are to change fundamentally in anyone's lifetime. On the other hand, it also shows how many stupid and reckless acts the human species has survived.

If the kind of vaguely worded "sexual harassment" codes that are springing up on college campuses around the country had been in effect in the garden of Eden, neither Adam nor Eve would have dared to make the first move—and there would be no human race today.

Wisdom from India: Never stand behind a horse or in front of an official.

I have never understood why businessmen consider it such an honor to serve on a college's board of trustees that they are prepared to condone dishonor in the way the institution is run.

People who talk incessantly about "change" are often dogmatically set in their ways. They want to change other people.

Boxing is the only sport where neither the athletes nor the spectators are told the score until after the contest is over. What sense does that make?

How can anyone read history and still trust politicians?

Self-respect is the most important thing. Without it, the world's adulation rings hollow. And with it, even venomous attacks are like water off a duck's back.

When you start to worry, you have to ask yourself: Is the worry itself doing more harm than the thing I am worrying about?

One of the best things about going to Harvard is that, for the rest of your life, you are neither intimidated nor impressed by people who went to Harvard.

Maturity is not a matter of age. You have matured when you are no longer concerned with showing how clever you are, and give your full attention to getting the job done right. Many never reach that stage, no matter how old they get.

Bad as it is financially for the federal government to be saddled with the runaway costs of "entitlement" programs, it is far worse for the society as a whole to be saddled with millions of people with the "entitlement" mentality and all the social problems that go with it.

No matter what you say, there are people who will hear only what they want to hear. Many of the heated political controversies of our times can be traced to that simple fact.

One of the most ridiculous defenses of foreign aid is that it is a very small part of our national income. If the average American set fire to a five-dollar bill, it would be an even smaller percentage of his annual income. But everyone would consider him foolish for doing it.

I am prepared to admit that the death penalty does not deter if the opponents of the death penalty can show me just one case where a murderer who was executed then committed another murder.

Isn't it amazing how rhetoric and zealotry can keep hysteria going about "overpopulation," at a time when so many nations around the world have chronic agricultural surpluses and overweight people?

Letters from teachers continue to confirm the incompetence which they deny. A teacher in Montana says that my criticisms of teachers are "nieve." No, it was not a typographical error. He spelled it that way twice.

Sometimes the Republicans seem to be machine-gunning themselves in the foot.

What a wonderful world this would be if there were as many wise people as there are clever people.

It is bad enough to see judges bending over backward and jumping through hoops for the sake of murderers. What is truly staggering is their indifference to the fact that decent, law-abiding people, who have been convicted of nothing, can have their children taken away from them for months without ever having seen a judge, a jury, or the inside of a courtroom—all this based on nothing more than the speculations of social workers.

People who insist that they have a right to their own opinions usually mean that they have a right to inflict those opinions on unwilling listeners. They also usually don't want to be confused with the facts.

If I could offer one piece of advice to young people thinking about their future, it would be this: Don't preconceive. Find out what the opportunities are.

Someone has said that human beings are the only creatures that blush—or that need to.

What do phrases like "glass ceiling" and "covert discrimination" mean, except that we are expected to accept claims without evidence?

Back in the heyday of the British Empire, a visitor from one of the colonies said to a London audience: "Please, do not do any more good in my country. We have suffered too much from the good that you have done already." That is my reaction to most of the liberal social programs for minorities and the poor today.

The rewriting of history has cast Republicans in the role of opponents of civil rights. But, when the landmark Civil Rights Act of 1964 and Voting Rights Act of 1965 were passed, a higher percentage of Republicans than Democrats voted for both bills in both houses of Congress.

Among the never-ending claims of discrimination is a recent charge that the game show "Jeopardy" discriminates against minority individuals who want to be contestants. This seemed particularly silly to me, since I was on "Jeopardy" before Alex Trebek was on "Jeopardy." I was a contestant back in the 1960s.

Some of the people on death row today might not be there if the courts had not been so lenient on them when they were first offenders.

When the end of the millennium arrives, someone may say: "It is the year 2000. Do you know where your country is?"

Even if we could make all the idiotic ideas and practices of our public schools magically disappear overnight, it would not do the slightest good, so long as the same shallow people were there the next day to find new idiocies to substitute for the hard work of teaching academic skills.

It used to be said that taxes are the price we pay to live in a civilized society. Today, taxes are the price we pay so that politicians can buy the votes of those who are feeding at the public trough.

Environmentalists love flattering themselves that trekking around in national parks is living in the wilderness. But this "wilderness" is presided over by a huge bureaucracy supported by billions of tax dollars and has in reserve everything from rescue helicopters to high-tech medical facilities. It is make-believe primitiveness, Disneyland for the anointed.

One of the worst examples of betrayal of trust are those judges who use the courtroom not as a place for enforcing the law and protecting the public, but as a stage for their own moral preening.

A reader who agrees with my impression that there are more good-looking women in the conservative movement than in movements on the left also suggests that this may be why more men are turning toward conservatism!

They say that love is blind. Nowhere is this more true than in love of jargon, which is one of the biggest obstacles to understanding.

What is so rare as a day in June? Common sense on the 9th Circuit Court of Appeals.

The American public schools' preoccupation with promoting "self-esteem" has been an overwhelming success. All sorts of people have tons of self-esteem, even when they are ignorant or incompetent.

Someone has come up with a sure-fire formula for making a small fortune in the oil business: Start with a large fortune and know when to quit.

People who believe in affirmative action have yet to explain why something that happened 40 years ago justifies discrimination against some guy who is 39.

When I think of all the genuine suffering in this world, I am offended by the fad of calling the ordinary vicissitudes of life "traumas."

The best obituary a man can have is that the people who knew him loved him, even if those who didn't know him hated him.

Too many people fail to see a distinction between "the rule of law" and the edicts of judges. Unfortunately, these people include many judges.

Liberals are horrified that the recently passed Republican welfare reform bill can force able-bodied people off welfare after two years. How many other Americans can live for two years without working?

My wife and I always agree in principle. For example, we both believe that things should not be put off until the last minute. We just disagree as to when is the last minute.

No one is more dogmatically insistent on conformity than those who advocate "diversity."

One of the most amazing examples of the childishness of our times is that so many individuals and groups think that they have a right to other people's favorable opinion—and that institutions or the government should punish or "re-educate" others who don't have a favorable opinion of them.

Many of the most fervent apostles of "informed consent" see no need for informed consent when it comes to judges changing the meaning of the constitution by "interpretations" that increasingly deprive the people of the fundamental right of self-government.

One of the mindless words of our times is "change." As someone has pointed out, there is always change—except from vending machines.

Did you know that a town in Montana has been named "Joe"?

A publication from New Zealand complains because New Zealand students rank below students from 14 other countries on international tests. Unfortunately, the United States ranks 14 countries below New Zealand.

Equal opportunity policies are against racism. Affirmative action is racism under new management.

Despite downsizing elsewhere, a recent study shows that we overweight Americans are now in the majority. Should we organize politically and have slogans like "Fat Power"?

Demagogues have always aimed their messages at the unthinking and the uninformed. Unfortunately, today that includes many of our college students.

To people who ask, "Why are we building more prisons instead of more schools?" the answer is simple: Prisons work and schools don't. Study after study has shown that even huge differences in spending on public schools make little or no difference in the quality of the education itself. Why should we allow criminals to walk the street while we create ever more expensive educational failures?

Everything has its good points. Even poison is non-habit-forming.

Know-it-alls really irritate me. Nobody knows even 10 percent of all.

Too many teachers today see their role as propagandists for the fashionable notions of the times. Their own "role model" is not Mr. Chips but Joseph Goebbels.

Whenever there is a proposal for a tax cut, media pundits demand to know how you are going to pay for it. But when there are proposals for more spending on social programs, those same pundits are strangely silent.

The only people I truly envy are those who can play a musical instrument and those who can eat anything they want without gaining weight.

Some people think that it is a strong argument for their side if they can cite a precedent for what they are advocating. But there are precedents for everything bad, from jay-walking to genocide.

Why do we keep getting panicked when we hear dire predictions from groups who are in the business of making dire predictions? Who would ever have heard about outfits like the Worldwatch Institute or the Center for Science in the Public Interest if they didn't go around constantly saying that the sky is falling?

I have no sympathy with parents who are embarrassed by their children's behavior in public. They should have raised them at home.

Insulating people from reality produces unrealistic people. It doesn't matter whether they are welfare recipients, spoiled rich kids, tenured professors in the ivy league, or federal judges with lifetime appointments.

Some say that the best defense is a good offense, so it is not surprising that parents who object to having their children brainwashed in the public schools are attacked for "censorship." What is surprising how often the schools get away with it because we don't bother to analyze what they are saying.

There is something obscene about judges and journalists nit-picking at leisure, and in safety and comfort, a life-and-death decision that some policeman had a split second to make.

Why does it seem to take longer to check out at cash registers, now that they have high-speed and high-tech equipment?

How can the same people say that it is morally and legally all right to have a racial spoils system today and yet that it was wrong to have had racial segregation and discrimination during the Jim Crow era? Is it just a matter of whose ox is gored? And were all the rest of us wrong to think that there was a moral principle involved?

One of the great mysteries of our time is why so many people who are either born rich or who gain great wealth in the media are so hostile to the values of American society and Western civilization. The most plausible explanation I have heard is that this stance enables them to enjoy their wealth with a clearer conscience as friends of the "underdogs" and enemies of "the establishment"—even though in reality they are really friends of parasites and enemies of civilization.

Some people justify their actions by saying "I have a right" to do this or that. We all have a right to do many things that it would make no sense to do.

Why do some restaurants play music more suitable for the young people who work there than for the middle-aged people who eat there?

Economists may not be able to cure our financial problems but their writings can cure insomnia.

Is it just my imagination or do these cold waves strike right after there has been a lot of talk about "global warming"?

One of the most heartbreaking statistics I have seen lately is that a quarter of a million Americans are emigrating from this country annually—and that one-fourth of all Americans earning over $50,000 a year have considered it.

After all the campaigns for "a drug-free workplace," former Republican White House press secretary Marlin Fitzwater refers to the city of Washington as "a work-free drug place."

The political left has never understood that, if you give the government enough power to create "social justice," you have given it enough power to create despotism. Millions of people around the world have paid with their lives for overlooking that simple fact.

According to the *Wall Street Journal,* a study of more than 3,000 witnesses testifying before Congress showed that most had themselves received federal money. Almost all of them advocated more federal spending.

Despite how often we hear race described as the worst source of hatred, the most hideous atrocities of our time have been committed by whites against other whites in the Balkans and blacks against other blacks in Africa.

One of the most ridiculous causes of automobile accidents is that some people are very eager to save very small amounts of time.

Letter from a working mother whose children are now grown: "Today we have our payoff. We live in a beautiful home and I drive a new Cadillac. I have literally everything I want. My husband buys me enormous gifts. People say we are rich. I would burn my house to the ground if I could go back to that day at the day care when I pulled away from clinging hands and cried all the way to work."

It is amazing how much time and ingenuity people will put into defending some idea that they never bothered to think through at the outset.

If you don't believe in the innate unreasonableness of human beings, just try raising children.

There are too many people who ought to be grateful for their good fortune, but who are arrogant instead.

Cheap behavior can turn out to be very expensive behavior.

Deception is one of the quickest ways to gain little things and lose big things.

One of the many signs of mushy thinking today is the claim that arguments against homosexuals or women in the military are parallel to arguments against blacks in the past. Think about it: The arguments against eating toadstools are parallel to arguments against eating tomatoes in the past. The only difference is that tomatoes don't kill nearly as many people as toadstools.

The number of expensive watches around always amazes me—especially since cheap electronic watches keep about as good time as the most expensive electronic watches.

Don't you get sick and tired of being propagandized and warned almost everywhere you turn? Someone said: "They are the missionaries and we are the Hottentots."

Time was when people used to brag about how old they were—and I an old enough to remember it. I can't claim to be old enough to remember when Moby Dick was a minnow. But I am old enough to remember when people trusted the government—which was almost as long ago.

Some people are fast asleep and slow awake.

Happiness is opening your bills on the first of the month and discovering that you have credit balances.

Perhaps it is just the generation gap, but I have never been able to understand the rush to get little toddlers out the door and into preschools and kindergartens. Phyllis Schlafly says, "the only thing you get in kindergarten is germs." Someone else said, "the earlier you institutionalize your children, the earlier they will institutionalize you"—in a nursing home, that is.

It is one of the pathetic signs of the "me generation" that some people think it is a defense of some government policy to say, "I benefitted from it." Nazis benefitted from Hitler!

Some people are such masters of the half-truth that it would be a waste of talent for them to lie.

One of the most dangerous trends of our times is that increasing numbers of people have a vested interest in the helplessness of other people.

When the history of corporate America is written, one of its most shameful chapters will be about how big business sold out to political correctness, by inflicting the harangues of "diversity consultants"

on their employees and donating their stockholders' money to advo-
cacy groups opposed to the free market on which their own existence
depends.

When you find yourself "keeping score" in a personal relationship,
that is a sign that you may lose the whole relationship.

Environmentalism is not about the environment. It is about ego trips
for busy bodies.